CERIL CAMPBELL

DISCOVER THE NEW YOU

CELEBRITY SECRETS TO TRANSFORM YOUR LIFE

DISCOVER THE NEW YOU

Copyright © Ceril Campbell 2007

All rights reserved.

Illustrations by Gina Adams

Layout by Rob Smith

The right of Ceril Campbell to be identified as the author of this work has been asserted in accordance with sections 77 and 78 of the Copyright, Designs and Patents Act 1988.

Condition of Sale
This book is sold subject to the condition that it shall not, by way of trade or otherwise, be lent, re-sold, hired out or otherwise circulated in any form of binding or cover other than that in which it is published and without a similar condition including this condition being imposed on the subsequent publisher.

Summersdale Publishers Ltd
46 West Street
Chichester
West Sussex
PO19 1RP
UK

www.summersdale.com

Printed and bound in Great Britain

ISBN: 1-84024-551-4
ISBN 13: 978-1-84024-551-6

Disclaimer

Every effort has been made to ensure that the information in this book is accurate and current at the time of publication. The book does not claim to include all information about all cosmetics and personal care products. The author and the publisher disclaim liability for any misuse or misunderstanding of any information contained herein and disclaims liability for all loss, damage or injury, be it health, financial or otherwise, suffered by any individual or group acting upon or relying on information contained herein. A qualified health practitioner should be consulted in all cases of ill health.

Contents

Part Three

Being Your Best You
How you can make the most of the new you:

Resources

Introduction

You would like to discover a new you. But how can you do it?

When you aren't happy with yourself and your life, but don't know how to change your circumstances, who can you talk to? Friends and family are often not those you wish to take advice from. You either won't listen to them, they won't listen to you, or they are too close to the problem. How do you find someone who can look deeper within you and strike a chord that you can relate to?

Maybe you don't want a dramatic change. Just a little tweak to your life. In the same way you might go to a spa to pamper yourself and give yourself a 'spring clean' or detox.

Wanting to change how you feel about yourself and how others perceive you can happen any time, whatever your age. This realisation could be a seed of thought that has gradually been growing over months or years, fuelled by a lack of self-esteem, weight gain or loss or an unhappy relationship. It could also be brought on by a sudden shock caused by betrayal, divorce, job redundancy, bereavement, illness, reaching a birthday milestone, empty nest syndrome or the loss of self-identity experienced by many new mums.

With the ever increasing pace of life, the instant fix is the easy option. Whether you choose the latest lunch hour plastic surgery that promises you a more youthful look, or Internet dating to find that elusive soul mate, neither solves the longer term issue of a life change. To be happy and self-fulfilled you need to discover *yourself* first.

How can you discover yourself?

I am going to help you. I will work with you, in the same way as I do with my celebrity clients, discovering who *you* really are, both your inner and outer you; finding out how you see yourself and how others see you, and how you can make small changes that may be invisible to others but that can make a big difference to you.

I will ask you a series of questions. My solutions for your 'best you' are based on your responses. So you will need to select responses that you most identify with and you will find your personal solution.

In this way you can continue your journey to 'discovering the new you' as though I am actually with you holding your hand all the way.

This is not a quick fix book but one where you will be taking a step-by-step journey with me, where the final destination is your best you. On the way you will be evaluating yourself and at various crossroads choosing the direction you want to take. This book is the vehicle for your journey of discovery with me. My aim is that when you have finished the book, you can continue on your journey with confidence on your own.

I have written this book drawing on my own experiences, on my one-to-one re-imaging work with personal clients and 25 years of styling celebrities. I have listened, watched and learnt about my clients' feelings about their body shape issues, self-doubts, lack of self-esteem, confidence, relationships and all the facets of how they feel about themselves and how others see them. You don't have to be perfect to make the most of yourself. As Elizabeth Arden said, 'Every woman deserves to be beautiful.'

My work has given me an insight into the psychology of feeling as good within yourself as you may appear to others. In my capacity as a celebrity stylist and image consultant the most amazing doors have been opened for me, giving me a chance not only to discover the beauty and style secrets of A list stars but also to work with them to hide their imperfections and insecurities.

I have met and worked with some of the most famous and glamorous people in the world, from sports stars to movie stars to royalty. Celebrities that I have styled over the years include Jane Seymour, Ringo Starr, Darcey Bussell, Anna Kournikova, Cat Deeley, Dannii Minogue, Katherine Jenkins and Princess Anne's daughter, Zara Phillips. I have been backstage at fashion shows and theatres; inside royal palaces; stayed in desert locations and five star hotels; walked down the red carpet and partied with stars, and been allowed to rummage inside celebrities' closets. My favourite closet was Ringo Starr's and his Beatles' vintage clothes.

It doesn't intimidate me to work with big name celebrities. I don't get easily overawed and when you do work with stars you realise that they are only human and have the same lack of self-esteem and feelings about their bodies as all of us.

In fact they are even more insecure as they're faced with the media picking apart their appearance.

Whether you're male or female, celebrity or not, looking good is not simply about being fit, stylish or wearing the latest designer label, but about attitude, confidence, and feeling good within, especially in your sexuality.

You don't have to be the best looking person in the room to attract or make people interested in you. But if you believe in yourself and feel good, you will exude an inner confidence and most importantly the magnetic power of attraction. This attraction is not about drawing people to you in a sexual way, but giving off a magnetic aura. If you are able to make people think that you are the most interesting person in the room, then you will be able to make new friends and business contacts for the future.

You can't expect to gain confidence and become a new person overnight, or even in a month, but you can improve on who you are in gradual steps.

Don't get overwhelmed by these steps to the new you. Once you feel good about yourself, anything is possible. Set yourself your new standards and small goals in baby steps, especially if you feel that you lost yourself somewhere along the way. Your goal could be, 'I will lose a few pounds by the end of this month' or, 'I will give myself an hour a day especially for me.' This hour could be to do anything, even just sitting doing absolutely nothing if you are constantly frantic during the rest of the day.

As soon as you start to invest in yourself, everything in your life will start to fall into place. If you water and nurture seedlings, they put down strong roots and become beautiful plants. In the same way, if you look after yourself you can become the 'new you'.

Ceril

x

Part One
The Inner You

How you feel about yourself and
how others perceive you:
the first stage of the journey
to the new you

Make the most of yourself, for that is all there is of you.

Ralph Waldo Emerson

On the first stage of your journey with me, I want you to find out how you *feel* about yourself. How you see yourself and how you think others see you. Do you just feel that you've lost your sense of style and you don't know how to dress for your age or for a changing body shape?

Or does your problem run deeper? How do you feel about the inner you and the outer physical you? Your personal relationships and your relationships with food, alcohol, shopping, exercise and even sex.

Do you say to yourself that you are always going to start that diet, give up smoking, or start the exercise regime tomorrow – never today? Do you always have excuses for yourself, or have these daily activities become addictions that create an adrenalin rush or a feeling of instant gratification?

Do you have low or no self-esteem and how and when did it disappear? Do you look in the mirror and say to yourself, 'I'm not worth it?'

You could find you have a completely distorted view of yourself. I have styled many celebrities who are beautiful and successful, but still have no self-confidence.

'I have exactly the same issues and hang-ups as any woman would have going down the red carpet. You know, what if I step on my train and tear my dress? What if I get my period? That's why a backup black dress is essential. When I read how an actress 'made a statement in black', I just think, "Oh, period or fat day." Sometimes you just don't feel confident enough to wear twinkly yellow taffeta.'

Kate Winslet

How can you define what is wrong with both you and your life that you'd like to change? How can you step outside your life and look in?

Try making lists with category headings. The first heading and column should include all those things that you like about yourself and your life. All those positive things you wouldn't want to change. Even if you can't find very many, there must be some. The second column should include those things that you are able to change that can make an instant difference. The third column should have all the things that you can change over time. Writing down your wishes and needs can often help clarify your thoughts.

'Ask the right questions if you're to find the right answers.'
Vanessa Redgrave

You can't wait for someone else to rescue you, or a life-changing solution suddenly to appear out of the blue. You are responsible for your own life and create your own destiny. If you want change in any area of your life, you are the only one who can make it happen.

It's a bit like an overgrown garden full of weeds. If you clear the weeds away creating space and light for new plant shoots they will have a chance to grow. With no light or space, they will

Positive things that you like about your life that you don't want to change	Things you can change that would make an instant difference	Things you could change over time
your children	de-clutter your life (e.g. rooms in the home, personal belongings, 'friends' in your address book)	look for a new job
your family	get a new haircut/colour	move house, move town
good eyes	get contact lenses instead of glasses	your whole body with exercise and a healthy nutritional diet
your sense of humour	put five minutes a day aside for 'you' time	improve your current relationship
good boobs	buy good underwear that makes you feel sexy	find a new lover/partner/ relationship
	go out more	
	find someone to babysit the children one night a week	

be suffocated and die. If you create the space in your life for new opportunities and possibilities for change, then these changes can have a chance to happen. In the same way de-cluttering your home could give it a whole new feel – maybe one that is more suited to your new life as the 'new you'.

If you confide in a close friend or someone you trust, sharing your thoughts and feelings, you may often find that you are not alone in those negative thoughts of how you feel about your body/your life/your partner or even your mortality. When you realise that there are others who feel the same, sometimes it helps you rationalise your thoughts. A negative head, or 'poor me' syndrome, will drag you down. Optimism will help you look ahead and see exciting new and positive things (however small) that happen to you each day, and you can build on them.

'Life is about creating new opportunities, not waiting for them to come to you.'

Salma Hayek

Be patient. It takes lots of little steps to make a long journey, in the same way as a day in your life is made up of lots of little details and events.

Q: How do you see yourself?

I'm worthless.

Have you let yourself go because you feel that you are worthless? Have you stopped taking any exercise and caring for your body, telling yourself, 'Why should anyone else be interested in me if I'm worthless?'

Have you immersed yourself in caring for your children to the exclusion of everything else? Do you think that they are the *only* ones that need you, and that takes the pain out of your meaningless existence?

How can you escape from this vicious circle that sucks you deeper and deeper each day into its vortex? As you are unhappy, you turn to food or alcohol. The more you eat, the fatter you become. You then look in the mirror and can't bear to look at yourself, become unhappier and repeat the cycle.

How can you break a pattern which may have been continuing for years? Has it gone on for so long that you can't see how to change it?

Or have you tried and failed already? Maybe you've given yourself too great a task. Maybe you expect a change in too short a time. If a problem has been continuing for years then you can't fix it in a day, a week or even a month. It needs to become a long-term plan taken in little steps; the equivalent of a great football goal, achieved with lots of little passes to get close enough to score safely.

I don't like myself.

Do you look in the mirror and hate what you see? What is it that you dislike? Is it your boobs, your tummy, or maybe your bum? Do you think you are too thin, too fat, disproportionate, too tall, too short? According to statistics, 50 per cent of you have low self-esteem and judge yourselves harshly, even if no one else is being critical of you.

Seeing and liking yourself is not about seeing your actual reflection in the mirror, but about how you perceive the whole of you from your personality to your body shape.

You need to accept the physical you. It's all about your mental attitude. If you think more positively then you will find that it's easier to move on with your life with renewed confidence.

You'll need to see yourself in a positive light to be able to turn things around and after years of negativity it can take a while to become positive again.

My husband or partner ignored me so I ignored my own needs.

You must always feel good and look good for *you*, not anyone else. But if you are constantly rejected, criticised or ignored it will be very difficult to regain confidence and step out of that helpless pit. But with the knowledge that only you can help yourself, it is important to remember that you owe it to yourself to tend to yourself and your needs, as you would weed and make over a neglected and overgrown garden. It might take time for the flowers to grow again and the

❝ If everybody's not a beauty, then nobody is. ❞

Andy Warhol

I'm uninteresting, unattractive, useless and unloveable.

Why don't you *like* you? Do you have a little voice repeatedly telling you that you're uninteresting, unattractive, useless, maybe even unloveable? Were these thoughts planted in your head by a partner, a family member or your school classmates from years ago? These thought patterns may have been reinforced with repetition over the years, gradually eroding your self-esteem.

How can you start to believe the positive and get rid of the negative?

lawn to look healthy and green but it will do, in the same way that you can look good again.

'If I hadn't been a fat teenager, I would never have been funny. If I had been as skinny as one of those supermodels I would never have developed my sense of humour.'

Joan Rivers

I hate my body!

Do you have a body image that you dislike enough to never undress in front of anyone, even your girlfriends or husband? Do you always undress in another room or in the dark? What is it that you don't like? Have you discussed it with your husband/partner/girlfriends? Would it be true to say that they all tell you that you look OK and your husband/partner keeps telling you how much he loves you and all the bits of you for who you are, but you still don't listen…?

The more you focus on those few parts of your body you do like and really listen to the positive reinforcement and compliments from your partner and friends, you may suddenly see the body that others see, not the one you conjure up in your mind.

I don't believe my friends and family when they say nice things about me.
Listen to your friends and family when they compliment you and accept it. If someone says how pretty you look, feel it! If you're praised for something you did, then realise that it *was* good. If someone writes you a letter complimenting you on something you did, keep it to read every time you feel lacking in self-confidence. They meant what they wrote in the letter.

I compare myself to others.
Challenge or compete with yourself but don't compare yourself to others. You would be surprised what others

may feel about themselves, however pretty or successful they may be. Most of the advertising images showing perfect women that you see daily have been digitally enhanced. Therefore, if you compare yourself to them, you will become more critical of yourself, with an unreasonable image and perception of how you feel you should look.

❝When you know all the world is going to see all your blobby bits, it's even worse. Some days you wake up feeling thin and pretty, other days you feel awful. I've got wobbly bits that I hate and I'm as embarrassed by my figure as any woman. I never feel gorgeous.❞

Joss Stone

But how many perfect women have you seen in reality? Maybe models in magazines and women under the age of 25, but I can guarantee that although you may perceive them as perfect, they too will be obsessing with at least one area of their bodies.

Every person whom I have ever styled, even the most glamorous Hollywood actress you see on the red carpet, has body shape issues. So let's look at the positive. What do you like most about yourself when you look in the mirror? Be realistic. You don't have to be perfect. The imperfections of the actresses and personalities you see on magazine pages have all been airbrushed out.

There must be something you can find to like about yourself… Your cleavage? How about your shoulders or your ankles? Focus on that area and make those who look at you do the same.

There is huge pressure for both women and men to look a certain way and use beauty products. You are supposed to be ultra thin, successful and look eternally youthful. You should aspire to the latest fashion trend, 'must have' handbag or Jimmy Choo shoe. Young girls are targeted by magazines to use the latest make-up, whilst women are being told to consider cosmetic surgery even when they are in their twenties.

We all want what we haven't got. We would like straight hair instead of curly, a big bust instead of small, and to be beautiful. But the grass isn't always greener. Many beautiful women feel cursed by their beauty, not blessed.

It's not easy to be beautiful, as often the most beautiful people are the most self-conscious, and always being stared at. Their looks may be their trademark, their life, their career. And as they age, they have to deal with losing their best asset.

Q: **How do you see your body shape?**

I worry about my body shape.
If you do, you are not alone. We seem to have reached a point where the word 'fat' is taboo and we are immune to true beauty, which can appear in all shapes and sizes.

'It feels like I have somehow fooled everybody and managed to cover up the misshapen strange child for an evening.'

Kate Beckinsale

Do you know what your body shape is, or do you simply know that you don't like it? But which part of your body is it that you don't like? Your boobs, your bum, the cellulite on your thighs or your actual body shape structure? Or do you feel that it's just all one big problem?

Your basic body shape is your skeletal make-up. You can change how thin or fat you are, but you cannot change your bone structure. You're stuck with it. But you can improve your body shape 'casing' by slimming,

toning, dealing with cellulite and looking after your skin. So put aside any thoughts of those bits you dislike and look again.

In Part Two, we will find out your body shape. Once you have established your shape, you can work on making the best of it with the styling, cut and colour of your clothes. Dressing cleverly can create an illusion of a different body shape. Knowing which shape you are can help you to look your best.

I can't bear to look in the mirror.
Do you hate what you have become so much that you never look in the mirror? Or even at yourself when you're in the bath? Your body may not be what it used to be, but there is no reason why

you can't improve it with exercise, good eating habits and body care. Yes, stretch marks happen with having children and everything gradually going south comes with age, but that's life and life is there to be lived. Just because your body isn't perfect doesn't mean than you can't still be attractive, even beautiful.

However slim you become, do you still see yourself as fat? Do you look at your body and actually hate it? Is sex always with the lights off? How can you overcome this problem which is all in *your* mind, especially if your body shape *in other people's eyes* is quite OK?

> *Someone with the perfect body may just be a bunch of perfect parts.*
>
> Matthew McConaughey

When you look in the mirror are you truthful to yourself and do you really see what you're looking at or are you in denial? Do you still see yourself as that size 10 woman you once were, when you're really now a size 16? Or do you see yourself as a fat woman, when it's only your tummy that carries the pounds and the rest of you is tall and slim?

Obviously you can't change your height or your bone structure but you can face reality and change how you perceive yourself. You may find that the reality could be better than the imagined you. Many of my clients who have achieved a significant weight loss still think of themselves as a few sizes bigger. They are really shocked when I select clothes the correct size which happen to be a few sizes less than they think they are.

Body dysmorphic disorder

Seeing yourself in the mirror not as your true size but as your imagined size (which to you may seem non-negotiable, however anyone tries to convince you otherwise) is a form of body dysmorphic disorder.

If you are anorexic, you may only see a fat person in the mirror, even if you only weigh seven stone. Equally, if you have low self-esteem you may imagine your body to be unattractive, when in reality it is perfectly acceptable.

It may be almost as if you are two different people. One is maybe the self you recognise from way back and the other is the self you find shocking to see in the mirror, as it is not the 'ideal' you have in your mind. To like yourself more you have to accept that *some* flesh/fat is essential. Wanting to be a better person is a positive thing, but wanting to be thinner will not make you a better person.

'I know I'm too thin right now, so I wouldn't want any young girl looking at me and saying, "That's what I want to look like." I started seeing a nutritionist and a doctor... I do recognise that I have a problem, and I want to be responsible and fix it, and I'm on that path right now.'

Nicole Richie

Most people with body dysmorphic disorder also have eating disorders, such as bulimia or anorexia. It may be that these psychological issues need to be resolved before you see yourself how others see you, so that you can see your true reflection in the mirror, not a distorted one.

I am having a 'feeling fat' day.

A fat day is not about how you look but about how you feel. No one else would actually see any difference in your body, but you could feel like a beached whale. Of course all women have times of the month when the body changes due to menstrual cycles, and maybe you do get water retention and carry an extra few pounds that week, but this is not a 'feeling fat' day. A feeling fat day is triggered by your insecurity, your lack of confidence and low sense of worth. Maybe you might be lonely, bored or dissatisfied. A feeling fat day can also be brought on by stress or a negative comment.

On these days you will imagine you see parts of your body seeming to be disproportionately large and think that everyone else is focussing on these parts too. Whether you target your tummy or your thighs as your fat parts, you'll decide to wear baggy or black clothes to cover them up and do extra exercise that day. These areas will become everything that you hate about yourself.

How can I stop having a feeling fat day?

Be aware that wearing baggy clothes, weighing yourself and checking yourself constantly in the mirror will make you feel worse. Be less judgemental and look at the things that you like about yourself that you know haven't changed from the preceding day, such as your eyes, your hair colour, your skin etc.

Stop imagining that everyone is only looking at your 'fat' bottom, thighs or your tummy. Could there be another reason they are looking? Perhaps because you have a great pair of legs or because you are tall and slim, or very attractive?

Try to remember to consider all your positive personal attributes and qualities and base your self-worth on those rather than your appearance. It will raise your self-esteem and confidence and those feeling fat days may eventually disappear or become less stressful and more manageable.

Can I change my shape with better posture?

With incorrect posture, you can reveal to others how you feel about yourself. If you have low self-esteem, it is very likely that you don't hold yourself proudly. Do you slump in your seat? Do you stand with your torso concertinaed into your hips, making your bust droop and tummy sick out? Or do you stand in an 'S' shape, with tummy and bum out and a sway back? Good posture can create a better body shape, lose pounds instantly and also make your body look better proportioned. If you stand up proud and pull up from your waist, you will look more confident and have more of a presence in a room.

If you are lacking in confidence from how you may have been treated by an ex-partner who was super-critical, it will be even more important for you to really look at yourself in the mirror and focus on the positive. No one is perfect.

How is your posture?

I hate my large bust and try to hide it by how I stand.

Even if you are self-conscious, shy or hate some part of your body, don't try to hide it with your arms or your stance. If you hate your large bust, don't stand slouched to try and hide it. You won't, you will only give yourself a droopy bust and sloping shoulders.

I slouch as I think I am too tall.

If you are tall, don't try to hide your height by standing slouched. Tall girls rarely stand tall as they were teased at school, so they carry on trying to look shorter. The shy young Princess Diana was an example of a young woman who began her public life with bad stance as she felt tall and also had a big bust. As she became more confident her posture changed and improved and she walked and stood tall, looking glamorous and self-assured, even if she wasn't feeling that way inside. Nicole Kidman commented after her split from Tom Cruise that finally she could wear heels again, as she had previously been so concerned about being taller than her man.

I try to hide my tummy.

If you feel your tummy is too large, don't sit with your arms crossed to hide it when you're seated. Try sitting up more and pulling it in instead. It will help remind your tummy muscles to get working again. If you have a short-waisted body shape, the more you stand up, the more it will lengthen the space between your chest and tummy. It will also lengthen a shorter neck, lift your bust (without surgery) and give you back a waist.

I lack confidence so maybe I subconsciously slouch.

Do you slouch and try to pretend you're invisible? Stand up straight, shoulders back with hips, knees and arms loose and eyes ahead. If you look relaxed and comfortable in your own skin, you will appear more confident and attractive.

 ## Are you obsessed by your weight?

I feel really fat.
Have you noticed a gradual weight gain that you felt you couldn't control? Do you have long-term unworn clothes hanging in your wardrobe, as they are for the other, thinner you? Maybe you do carry a few excess pounds, have boobs that have drooped, or a tummy that bears the tale of your pregnancies. But don't imagine that your current partner or future partner will focus on this area when they look at you, as they won't. They will simply see the whole you and like or love you unconditionally for who you are. The most beautiful celebrities have insecurities about all sorts of parts of their body, even body parts that most of you wouldn't begin to consider a problem!

'I don't like my hands because my knuckles are too big. If I get married, I'm worried that the ring won't fit.'
Eva Longoria

However much exercise I do I can't shift those last few pounds.
You should never weigh yourself every day as your weight will fluctuate according to the time of the month and what you ate the preceding day, and even if you've been to the loo! Muscle weighs more than fat and as you have been losing fat by exercise you will have been gaining muscle. Instead you should look at yourself in the mirror undressed and then try on your clothes. How they fit will tell you how your weight loss is progressing. You may find that you actually don't need to lose those extra pounds. You are absolutely fine as you are. There are many celebrities who are in denial about their weight. Try to see you as you really are. If you think you may have an eating disorder, it is important to seek help.

Have you ever asked yourself why you're eating, when you're not actually hungry? Is snacking your only treat? Is eating the only time you let yourself be out of control? Does eating fire up your senses and become a sensual or gratifying experience? When you do give into your cravings and needs, do you feel the need to binge? What else have you left yourself to enjoy? If you have an addictive personality, when you give up something it's likely that you will find an alternative addiction. So you need to find a balance.

It's all about being less hard on yourself and allowing yourself a small amount of those things you crave within reason, without completely cutting them out. It shouldn't be an all or nothing scenario. That's why diets never work. You should be able to enjoy a small bar of chocolate once a week or an occasional glass of wine without beating yourself up.

So how do you change your mindset about food so that *you* use *it*, instead of *it* using *you*?

I eat when I'm unhappy, stressed or just bored.

You need to be aware what triggers your desire to eat when it's not hunger driven, and find something that occupies that moment instead. You probably need to make sure that you are as far away from

> ❝ *One of the best exercises for losing weight is the "push-yourself-away-from-the-dining-room-table-before-you-eat-too-much" exercise.* ❞
>
> Joan Collins

Q: How is your relationship with food?

Is food your friend? But what sort of friend? One you turn to when you're depressed or stressed? Or is it more of an addictive or abusive relationship? You should know when to walk away from any abusive relationship and get help. In the same way, you should be able to enjoy your food and walk away, still leaving some on your plate.

Everyone is human and everyone has imperfections and emotional vulnerability. So why try to be perfect? Be kinder and more forgiving on yourself and you may find that you don't need to seek the comfort of the food, alcohol or drugs or even shopping that you may use to dull your possibly unacknowledged inner pain.

the kitchen or food temptation as possible. Try going out for a short brisk walk (as exercise helps produce the endorphins or happy feelings). Or even have a chat on the phone with a friend. Anything that helps distract you from the instant gratification that eating will give you.

I think if I eat I will put on all my weight again.

You need to understand why and when you eat. Always have breakfast. It sets you up for the day. If you need a mid-morning snack and you really know you aren't able to control your urge for only one biscuit, don't have any at all and substitute for an alternative healthier nibbling choice. Always try to exercise before you eat a meal as the exercise will raise your metabolism. When you eat you will burn up the calories quicker.

Shaping up, starting to exercise

How do you get in the mindset to start exercise? Once you start and create some semblance of a routine, even if it's only 20 minutes a few times a week, you will find that the action of exercise triggers off endorphins and you will start to feel good about yourself after the exercising. As the weeks pass you will see the changes in your body which can only serve to make you feel even better about yourself. Looking good is all about feeling good which comes from within. So in the end, it doesn't really matter what size you are as long as you feel good about how you look. It's unlikely that you need to be as toned as Madonna, who apparently does three hours a day. You only need to be fit enough to have a flatter tum, a perkier bum and eliminate those under-arm bingo wings.

See Part Two for more about starting to exercise.

Q: Do you feel depressed?

I feel depressed as I have no confidence or self-esteem.
If you lack self-esteem, however many times your friends tell you that you're pretty, you still aren't going to believe them. You will still see yourself as that unattractive person in your mind.

Maybe you had a prettier, cleverer, older sister, or a more handsome, higher achieving, older brother, or parents that had a higher expectation of you than you felt you could ever achieve. Or conversely parents who didn't care. So how can you increase your confidence? How can you see what others see in you? Try not to compete with anyone other than yourself and each time you succeed in something, give yourself a mental point as a reward. This success could be anything from finally getting into that pair of jeans you bought that were too tight, to attracting someone you've been fancying for ages, or jogging for ten minutes longer than usual. You will soon find those points keep clocking up, and the sense of achievement will boost your inner confidence.

Being at home depresses me.
If you can't get out, then you will feel feel trapped and therefore depressed. Even a five minute breath of fresh air and quick walk round the block will help renew your energy. Some sort of exercise will help elevate your mood. Also being in and seeing sunlight/daylight will help, especially if you live in a dark home.

Is your home too small? Maybe de-cluttering would help, as it will make the rooms seem bigger. Redecorating a dark, dingy room to be a light, bright one will make it much less depressing.

If certain rooms do make you feel depressed, it could be the colour of them that is affecting how you feel. Certain colours will be more uplifting. Yellow creates a sunshine-happy feel, whilst red creates energy. Blues, greens and lilacs are tranquil and calming. A bedroom should always be a calming and peaceful coloured environment, helping you to sleep peacefully.

Self-esteem

How do you feel about yourself? Do you have self-esteem? Do you like who you are or do you feel that you are worthless and unattractive? Self-esteem is the most important thing that you can have. With self-esteem it doesn't matter what anyone else says or does to you as you are secure in the knowledge that actually you are OK. It isn't about how you look or how successful you are but just about the value you put on yourself.

When you value yourself you have the confidence to be yourself, not to be a victim, to stand up to your bullies and to take control of your life and empower yourself.

I am stuck in a hopeless rut.
When you feel that you are stuck in a rut, how can you escape? Is the problem how you think you look, how you interact with people, or do you feel that your life is going nowhere?

So, what's your goal? Could you make a plan of action and achieve it? It doesn't have to be instantly attainable but should be something that could gradually happen over time, with little baby steps.

How about making another table? It could cover the various aspects of your life that need a change, i.e. home, family life, work, clothes, body and exercise, social life, love life. Under each heading you could then put all the things that you would like to change over time.

This list could contain anything, however small – even if it seems stupid, it may make a big change to YOU.

'Men do not stumble over mountains, but over mole hills.'
Confucius

So how can you meet more people who can become new friends, or present yourself in a different way?

You should start to make the most of your contacts. Learn to network. Take care with how you dress and what first impression you give. You don't need to be the smartest or most talented person in the room to get ahead but if you sound confident enough, people will listen to you and believe in you.

It's important always to be optimistic and never lose hope. You need to be a glass half full person, not half empty. There is always tomorrow to pick yourself up and start again if today wasn't good.

Home	Family life	Social life
Tidy bedroom and wardrobes (not a difficult task – just something that maybe you keep putting off)	Husband or friend/relation to do school run once a week to give you a break	Go and learn a new skill whilst making new friends.

Q: **Is your lack of self-esteem connected to your personal relationships?**

I use sex to gain self-esteem.
Do you sleep with a man to make yourself feel desirable? It may make you feel wanted at the time, but it's the same as eating a large bar of chocolate.

It only felt good while it lasted: a quick fix and then you felt empty again. You don't need a man to boost your confidence and prove to yourself that you are desirable and not a worthless human being. That knowledge of self-worth can only come from your inner you. You can't look to others to be your prop.

Mental bullying has erased my self-esteem.

Are you being bullied? Do you forgive the bully (because you love them) each time they apologise? Do you only see their good points while all the time your self-esteem is being eroded?

It's common to lack self-esteem after being bullied as a child at school, as an adult in your workplace or in your own home by your partner. Bullies always pick on the vulnerable, as they know that they will not be challenged. Many bullies are those who are the weakest and pick on others to make themselves feel better. Mental bullying can often be subliminal and you may not realise that it is even happening at the time. It could be that your partner always undermines you. He or she may never reciprocate any loving or tenderness or worse still refuse or rebuff your sexual approaches. Any of these things will gradually erode your self-esteem, however strong it may have been in the beginning. Everyone needs some sort of confirmation or approval. It could be from your parents or your partner but repeated negativity will breed lack of self-esteem.

It's very difficult to ignore repeated criticism, especially if it is always negative. But if you can be aware of it, without taking it to heart, then you can decide over a period of time what you wish to do to address the problem. Do you have the confidence or means to walk away or escape from the person or situation? Or do you stay? A verbally abusive relationship can be as destructive as a physically abusive one.

I no longer have sex, as he doesn't seem to fancy me any more.

Have you been with your partner for what seems an eternity and does sex no longer seem to be on the agenda? Does your partner tell you he no longer finds you attractive, or has fallen out of love with you? If you no longer have sex you may find that you argue more often, are likely to be more irritable and depressed, and will start to lose your self-esteem.

Regular sex within a loving relationship, even if it's a quickie, can help a relationship stay the course. It can help you communicate, show affection and be energised. Everyone needs some bodily contact, even if it's only a hug.

When you have a problem in a relationship, it is very easy to get stuck in a cycle of blame and shame. Have you considered that you could also be responsible for the problems? Try to look at the problems from the outside.

'I want a man who's kind and understanding. Is that too much to ask of a millionaire?'

Zsa Zsa Gabor

Do you blame yourself or your partner? Perhaps you may be partly to blame, maybe you didn't pay enough attention to him because of your children or work pressures. It takes two to make a marriage or partnership work. The more you put into a marriage the more you get back. Have you lost who you were along the way and are no longer a lover and friend to your partner?

This book will encourage you to remember who you once were, and who you can be again. If you can rediscover yourself, you will be better equipped to regain a loving relationship.

❝I believe that everyone is the keeper of a dream – and by tuning into one another's secret hopes, we can become better friends, better partners, better parents, and better lovers.❞

Oprah Winfrey

Q: **How do you think others see you?**

I don't know.

Have you ever considered how others see you? Do you think you see yourself in the same way as they do or would you be upset if they told you their view? When told how they see you, would you withdraw into yourself, or be shocked and try to change accordingly? Do you take criticism personally or is it water off the proverbial duck's back? So who can you ask the questions 'How do I appear to you? What did you think of me when you first met me?' Who can you trust to give you the truth, or at least an unbiased opinion? If you have close platonic friends of the opposite sex, try them first. You may be pleasantly surprised to hear what positive things friends of the opposite sex have to say about you. You may get a more generous reply from a man than one of your female friends.

There is often an underlying element of competition from your same sex friends – call it survival of the fittest. You could be amazed at how even your best friends may be jealous of some aspects of your life, and therefore be more economical with the truth. But make it clear when you ask that you want the truth, nothing less. However good or bad the feedback is, it can only be positive, as you then have knowledge about yourself to work with.

I don't think they notice me.

Why don't you think you are noticed? Do you choose to dress in colours and styles to be invisible and to purposely fade into the background, or do you feel that you don't have the personality or looks to be noticed?

Or did your mother constantly criticise you and tell you, as you were growing up, that you weren't good looking, that you should lose weight or drop hints about your acne?

You need to believe in what you now see in the mirror and not listen to those old voices in your head. If you were that scrawny bespectacled gangly teenager, or the one with the acne-covered face you couldn't hide, or the fat girl in the class... look again. That's not who you *now* see in that mirror. Don't let that image be reflected back at you. Others were ugly ducklings too – it's up to you to see yourself as a beautiful swan.

It is important to be noticed. You may not want to be noticed in an obvious way, but you don't want to be ignored. You need to

> **Deep down I'm pretty superficial.**
>
> Ava Gardener

be noticed to leave a positive impression. First impressions are important in this fast paced life we live, so it's vital that you present the best 'you' possible. The first impression that you give may influence a prospective employer, a new hot date or just making new friends.

I don't want to be noticed.

Are you so shy that you can't bear to draw attention to yourself? Are you worried that everyone is judging your every move, what you wear and what you say? If so, how can you overcome this state of mind?

Firstly you have to realise that many people are actually far more interested in themselves than others, and will be looking out for themselves as a result. So it's very likely that they won't have noticed that you blushed when introducing yourself, as their attention may have moved on already.

Are they judging what you wear? Possibly, because first impressions count... but turn it around in your mind... do *they* look that great? They may well be as shy as you but just hiding it better. It's always good to see things from the point of view of others. It helps you feel better about yourself.

Are you terrified of meeting someone because they are important? Remember that everyone is the same underneath, however famous. Try imagining them on the loo – it will help divert you from your shyness issues!

Others see me as confident and successful, but I'm not.

Have you dedicated your whole adult life to the pursuit of career success, to reaching beyond the glass ceiling? But at what cost?

Often business colleagues see you as confident and successful, but in reality you are shy. You can still be driven, ambitious and a perfectionist but with low self-esteem.

To be a high achiever you are often a perfectionist. When you're a perfectionist you are self-critical and do not take criticism well from others. Many high achievers don't feel that they are successful. They are also often the outsiders and feel the need to prove themselves with drive and the relentless pursuit of a goal or challenge. But this pursuit of achievement does not bring happiness, and often it even brings loneliness.

Did you lose your friends, your social life and who you are along the way? Do you live for your work and not work to live? If you were to lose your job or get sick what would you have then? Does it make sense to work that hard if you have no one to share it with, or to talk with about your successes and your failures or discuss those funny moments in your day? It's important to re-evaluate your life every so often and decide if what you're doing is what you really want.

Are you really happy? You won't know until you try an alternative and you are the only one who can change your situation. And it's never too late to do so. If you can be that successful at work, there is no reason why you can't have as much success with your personal life. It's all about giving yourself a chance.

They see me as a loser.

Who told you that? No one! (And if they did, should you believe them?) So why do you think that you're a loser? Consider the positive things about yourself (remember the chart you did earlier?). Consider your kindness, your honesty or hard work ethic, or even your best assets such as breasts or your hair.

No one is simply a loser, only in the movies. Yes, life can work against you and everyone has their ups and downs. You may not be the best looking, the most successful, the thinnest or the richest, or you may just have been

'In every aspect of our lives, we are always asking ourselves, "How am I of value?"'

Oprah Winfrey

Are you overly critical of yourself and how others see you? Are you too harsh on yourself or on in your judgement of others? Maybe you are an only child and feel under pressure to be as perfect for your parents as possible. An only child is the focus of all your parents' attention and hopes. Only children are usually the highest achievers, perfectionists and over critical of themselves. It's difficult to stop being so self-critical, but if you understand that you don't have to be perfect all the time, life will only become easier.

Q: So who are you?

You may feel differently about yourself tomorrow. We all have a different view

'No one can make you feel inferior without your consent.'

Eleanor Roosevelt

made redundant or sacked from your job, but that does not make you a loser. Take Frank Spencer in the old TV series *Some Mothers Do 'Ave 'Em*. Whatever he attempted to do always went wrong, but he was endearing, loveable and always well-intentioned and he and his wife Betty really loved each other.

and priorities according to what stage of life we are at. Babies expect feeding. Children want to play. Teenagers want sexual experimentation. Young adults think they are immortal. Middle-aged people look back on their youth and wonder where the years went. Everything changes all the time just as you do, so however bad you perceive your life or current situation to be, it will be changing again very soon.

I only see myself as a mum.
Have you forgotten who you are? Do you only see yourself as your children's mum, not as 'you'? And do others, including your partner, only see you as a mum too, not as that attractive, sexy woman you were when you first met (and still are)? Or have you forgotten how to be sexy? Have you forgotten that you have a partner who might find you attractive and would like to interact with you as you once were? Do you find time to do this? It is very important to be able to remember who you are and find time for yourself and also time to be a wife and lover. However frenetic your life may be, there is always a way (even if it means calling upon your family or friends to help with your kids) to put aside even one night a week.

Bringing up children is never easy, and although always rewarding, it can be emotionally, physically and financially draining. It's easy to become all-consumed by your kids and forget you ever had a life. You may have let yourself go, with the excuses to yourself that you have no time, your children need you 24/7, no one will ever fancy you again or you just aren't interested in men any

more. But these are excuses, not reasons to hide away. One day your children will be grown-up and won't need you any more and then where will you be? Probably feeling lonely and abandoned and wondering where the years went. So it's time to get out of the home and start balancing your life, even if it's only for a few hours a week. You will start to remember what life was like, pre-kids.

I only see myself as my parent's carer.
Do you hanker after freedom and being answerable to no one? To lead a purely selfish, self-indulgent life as maybe you once did? But no one can ever be free of dependants of some sort. Parents, in their old age needs, become like your children. It's important to be always there for them, but to keep some time for yourself. Even if only for a few hours twice a week in the evening. It's about making a few small rules and boundaries for yourself that you keep to, so you can retain a breathing space for yourself without being suffocated and still give a fulfilled life to both you and your dependants.

'The worst part of success is to try to find someone who is happy for you.'
Bette Midler

Re-invention

Do you believe in yourself? If you believe in yourself, others will. Don't wait for someone else to endorse or confirm your worth. It's all about what messages you give off. Many celebrities and pop stars such as Kylie or Madonna are masters of re-invention. Re-invention also helps to keep you feeling and looking younger as you will not be stuck in a rut. You can look older than your biological years by never progressing from that 20 years ago style moment or equally trying to dress 20 years younger than you are. There is no reason why you can't look a stylish ten years younger than your real age (see 'Dressing for your age' in Part Two).

Q: Would you like to look ten years younger?

'I love walking fast. That way nobody can see my wrinkles.'
Anita Roddick

How old do you look? Your biological age? Possibly even older? Would you like to look younger? Looking younger does not need to be created by plastic surgery. It's about your outlook on life, how you carry yourself, stand, speak, and wear your clothes, hair and make-up. Of course plastic surgery can transform, as can non-surgical procedures such as Botox and non-surgical facelifts and peels, but the *inner you* is the one that has to change first.

I feel that I have wasted my life so far and now it's too late.
Do you feel that you are past your sell-by date? Have your best years gone? If Sophia Loren at 72 can be considered sexy enough to do a photo shoot for Pirelli then there is hope for all of us that it is never too late to start over.

I'm thinking about cosmetic surgery.
With all the TV coverage of cosmetic surgery procedures and the trend for thinking that a nip and a tuck can change your life, it's important to realise that actually it won't. Of course bigger bosoms will make you initially more attractive to certain men and a facelift may well take ten years off, but you are still the same you inside. If you do make these changes, you will need to learn how to adapt to the shift of the perception of you. Many of the TV cosmetic surgery makeover subjects are often rejected by their neighbours and friends and even partners after the transformation. When the outside persona no longer matches the inside, your old friends and relations may find it hard to reconcile the new you with the old one. You may do too. That's why the TV makeover subjects are often offered therapy and counselling.

6 *When you walk around New York or LA, everyone looks the same. It's pathetic. The lips all look like duck lips, there's no more wrinkles, the noses are all identical, and everything that made someone beautiful has gone. I know what it feels like to think you need to mutilate yourself. I thought, "Maybe if I stick some fake breasts on, it will be OK." But when I hit my sixties I felt so ashamed.* 9

Jane Fonda

Q: **Do you ever have any 'you time'?**

I have too much to do to look after myself.
If you have too much to do, try to prioritise and focus on the most important things. Maybe some things really don't need to be done today. Maybe you are taking the weight of the world on your shoulders. Try to delegate, even if it means your partner of your children doing something they would never usually do. Your children may enjoy being given a grown-up seeming task if they are young, and if they are older, then they could possibly help you more anyway.

Are you trying to be all things to all people? Are you trying to be a good mother, wife, lover, daughter, friend, business woman and more? You may look great from the outside as you look successful, happily married with all material wants and needs satisfied. But are you living on adrenalin, coffee and stress? This is equivalent to running a car on no petrol. You will get ill and then what will happen?

I never have any time for me.
Does everyone always need you? If so, make sure they really can't get hold of you whilst you take some 'you' time doing something that you really enjoy. Maybe it's just watching a soap on TV.

It doesn't matter what it is if it makes you happy.

Do you often feel alone, even when you're surrounded by people? Do you keep yourself so busy that you don't have to think about what's wrong? Life is different now from how it was 50 years ago. Fewer people live within a community or with a family support system around them. Many of us have relocated for that better job, or as a result of a marriage break-up, and can feel very isolated. When you are alone (and you can feel alone even if you have children whom you are close to, as you need adult company too), you can immerse yourself in your job or your children with no 'you time'. But you need 'down time' to concentrate on your wants and needs and re-energising yourself.

This time will enable you to escape from the treadmill of your everyday life and give you a break, even if only once or twice a week. It could be something simple and mundane or as far removed from your real life as you like, even if it seems mad to you at first. It could be something you always wanted to do. Maybe vary your days, take a different method of transport to work, take time for a quick coffee/gossip with a girlfriend, or stop off after work for a drink somewhere you've never been before with a work colleague. You never know who you could meet or what could happen. It could be fun.

Some suggestions:

• Reading a new book or a magazine
• Learning to play the piano or guitar
• Singing lessons
• Joining the local amateur dramatic society
• Giving yourself a home beauty or spa style treatment, including a proper manicure or pedicure
• A walk
• If you never normally cook, looking in a cook book and trying to cook a new dish, or even a cake
• A window shopping expedition
• Yoga
• Getting a dog. You'll *have* to take time out for both yourself and the dog to walk it twice a day and you will get exercise into the bargain.

I feel guilty and selfish putting myself first.

Do you feel guilty putting yourself first? This is normal, especially when you emerge from a long term relationship. Do you only feel worthwhile when you feel needed? But being needed isn't the same thing as being loved… Do you find yourself repeating patterns whereby you are attracted to needy and childlike men? Do you try to feel better in yourself and gain self-esteem by giving in to their needs and demands and trying to make them feel better? You must be responsible for your own feelings and they must be responsible for theirs. You are an independent adult, not an emotional prop. Although, if you do care mutually for someone, then the relationship should be a two-way street where you both offer support to each other but neither becomes a crutch.

How you care about yourself determines the quality of your life. You need to put yourself first to have enough energy to care for others. Even an occasional ten minute time out for yourself will help improve your quality of life. By being good to yourself, you can bring out the best in others.

I feel guilty when I sit down to relax.

You need to recharge your batteries, otherwise you will be irritable, forgetful, feel constantly tired and crave foods that give you a quick fix of energy. Slow down, you only have one life. If you do slow down, you might find you can prioritise and find those things that are truly important to you.

'If there's no inner peace, people can't give it to you. The husband can't give it to you. Your children can't give it to you. You have to give it to you.'
Linda Evans

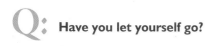

Have you let yourself go?

I've no time or no money.

Do you neglect your personal grooming because you don't have time or money, or because you don't feel a need as there is no one else to see you? Grooming and keeping your body in the best shape possible will make you feel your best. Just because you may not have a boyfriend doesn't mean that you don't need to shave your legs, or have a bikini wax. Hair colour should be kept up, with roots being re-touched and a haircut to suit your age and face shape. If money is short choose a colour and cut that is low-maintenance. Looking good is all about feeling good from the inside, and that means that you should feel good about your whole body under the covering of clothes in the same way as a sexy set of underwear will make you feel sexier even if no one else sees them.

I've had a serious illness and have lost the incentive to look good anymore.

How do you come to terms with a life-threatening disease such as breast cancer that can leave your family and loved ones on their own? If the disease is caught early enough, together with a positive attitude and the best medical treatment, how do you feel once in remission? Do you feel that others treat you differently when you only want to be treated the same as you were before?

Even if it appears on the outside that you have everything to live for, together with the support of a loving family, it doesn't mean that you feel the same way about yourself inside, even though you may have been granted that precious second chance of life. You may feel that having faced the possibility of death, thinking about how you look is totally shallow. You may feel that no one will even fancy you anyway post-mastectomy. But it's important to remember that looking good is part of being alive and feeling good.

I had a serious accident and I feel that my life has come to an end due to the scarring.
Do you really feel that your life has come to a full stop? Do you think that new friends will only see your disfigurement or scarring? And what will your old friends say or do? They may be initially cautious and shy in what they say to you, but will accept you in the same way as they knew you before, as they will only see the old you. Maybe your

> **❝ I don't look too bad for someone my age, with my history of illnesses and operations and all those anaesthetics. When they knock you out, it gives you time to catch up on your beauty sleep. ❞**
>
> **Elizabeth Taylor**

You owe it to both yourself and your partner and family to look your best, now that you are feeling well and are well. Why dwell in the past? Look forward. Why not feel proud of yourself for conquering the disease and also feel proud of yourself for how you now look too? Take Kylie as a role model. You will give yourself back your self-esteem when you feel good and both you and your family will benefit. Face the world and take it on.

confidence will have taken a knocking, but now it's even more important to concentrate on using that power of attraction, of using your personality and charisma, drawing their eyes and attention to the best bits of you. In that way your new friends will be drawn to you whatever your disability.

'I cried myself to sleep wishing I was ugly because men leered and disrespected me.'
Evangeline Lily of *Lost*

Everything has gone downhill since I reached the menopause.

With what do we associate women's menopausal symptoms – a new toy boy boyfriend? It's more likely to be the hot sweats, flushes and an apple-shaped middle-aged spread for most of us. For both sexes it's also the thought that half your life is now past and that youth is behind. But since 50 is the new 40 there is no reason why being menopausal or post-menopausal should mean a major life change. At least you may not have to worry about birth control any more. So sex should be more enticing, not less. Nowadays with the correct nutrition and hormonal support if necessary, most women should be able to breeze through with few symptoms. There is no reason to let yourself go.

You may have found that your body has become more curvaceous, with more flesh mostly in the wrong places, but you may also have a bigger bust. So why not look at the bright side. This could be the first time you've had a bust since you were pregnant!

I have passed my best years.
There is something positive to be gained and enjoyed from each period of your life. Yes, you may not look so youthful any more but look at the knowledge and experience you now have. You will attract admirers with your aura and personality and conversation as much as superficial youth and beauty.

Fifty-somethings like Twiggy, sixty-somethings like Helen Mirren and seventy plus like Lauren Bacall all look wonderful and are ambassadors for how to look stunning for your age. Yes, they are celebrities, with the money and access to the best beauty and style advisors and therapists but they have all been through the menopause too. Everyone, however famous, has the same bodily functions. So look forward to the next part of your life.

'If I could go back in a time machine and talk to myself aged 25, I'd say this: 'Don't waste your time on being shy. Don't let anyone sap your self-esteem. You're beautiful, intelligent and talented, so don't let the bastards get you down.'

Joan Collins

Q: **Now that you have journeyed through the first stage of questions about how you feel about yourself, how would you like to change?**

I would like to be more assertive, and more confident.
I would like to look better and more stylish.
I would like to get a new life.
You can have all this, as you create your own destiny. Things don't just happen. You have to make them happen.

So how do you do that?

Don't be one of life's victims. Be proactive and make small changes step by step.

Create a mental picture of the new you that you would like to be, say, in a year's time and then in a few more years' time. Imagine that 'new you' living the life you would like and being that person you never thought you could be. But it has to be achievable, don't be unrealistic. Then it will actually work.

In Part Two of the journey you can find out how you can change the physical you, with clothes, beauty and make-up tips, healthy eating and exercise.

'Vitality shows in not only the ability to persist but the ability to start over.'
Scott Fitzgerald

❝I refuse to become part of this perfect body syndrome. I like my body. It looks good on-screen, and it's not because it's perfect. I accept it and wear it like a good dress... One guy I dated said: "You're beautiful but you're soft. You can't compete with other actresses in Hollywood because everyone's in shape and working out." I said: "Very nice to meet you. Goodbye!"❞

Salma Hayek

Part Two
The Outer You

How you can change yourself physically:
the second stage of the journey to the new you

Individuality is beautiful. Old, young, skinny, curvy. I love a face with lines on it. We should work with what we have and make the best of it.

Liv Tyler

Now that we have looked at how you feel about yourself, what would you like to start changing about yourself?

This section covers how you can change any part of the *physical* you from top to toe, using my celebrity beauty, fashion, make-up and exercise tips and suggestions of non-surgical beauty procedures.

You will be able to find out how you can change or improve your problem areas but most importantly come to terms with whatever shape you actually are. Imagine I am with you in your home, talking about you and your life. We have discussed how you feel about yourself and how you feel others perceive you. Now we are going to talk about looking your physical best.

How would you like to be perceived on first impression? All it takes is 30 seconds for someone to make an initial judgement of you, so first impressions are important. A first impression is what you give off overall – a combination of your personality, confidence, posture, body language, voice, eye contact, and also hair, make-up, clothes, accessories.

The mix of the inner and outer you gives someone a way of assessing you, before getting to know you properly.

The outer you is as important as the inner you as it is part of what makes you unique. So let's start with making the best of the outer you. We will start at the head and work down to your toes!

'Rail thin models might look good on the runway, but it's women with curves and a butt who look good in real life'

Donatella Versace

Face

❛*Men become much more attractive when they start looking older. But it doesn't do much for women, though we do have an advantage: make-up.*❜

Bette Davis

Most of the celebrities I have styled over the years have had top make-up artists working with them to help them look their absolute best. Celebrities, like all of us, have their 'feeling ugly' days with bad skin moments, major spot outbreaks, puffy eyes, dark shadows, skin allergies and more. But the final images we see of them are of flawless perfection, due to the expertise of make-up artists and also the wizardry of the magazine art department digital re-touching. So we tend to forget that even celebrities are human and however beautiful they are, their imperfections need covering up with make-up just as ours do.

The celebrity has to have absolute trust in both the make-up artist and the stylist (myself), to create an image that gives her confidence and makes her feel transformed from her own inner perception of an ugly duckling to her public image of the beautiful swan. You would not believe how many celebrities have major insecurities and confidence crises before appearing in public or in front of a camera. To look beautiful you have to feel beautiful as beauty begins within.

According to a survey of 5000 women, only one in 20 of you feel confident without make-up. As many as 80 per cent said you don't leave home without wearing it, mostly because you believe it makes you look sexier and feel 'happier with life'. You spend almost an hour a day using beauty products and would give up other essentials and treats such as food, nights out, cars and holidays to be able to buy your favourite products.

'I'd asked my mother what she did in the war when her flat had been blown up. She remembered taking a bottle of Shocking perfume, by Schiaparelli. She said, When there's nothing left, you stick to the superfluous.'

Jane Birkin

Buying make-up and the anticipation of putting it on can make you feel good. You can wake up looking and feeling rough and even with a minimal application of products you can become an improved you in less than five minutes.

All the make-up products I mention here, I have tried and tested personally, or have used on my clients. I have listed them in order of how I would apply them if I were doing your make-up. Creating a make-up look is a gradual build-up of effect. Each item will have its own job to do, but will balance another. Doing make-up is like decorating a room. You have to prime the walls and fill the cracks before painting. Once you have the whole room painted uniformly, then you can start adding the furniture and colour touches with cushions, curtains and accessories. Each time you add a chair or a cushion you need to stand back and look at how it affects the balance and proportions of the room space. In the same way, the foundation is your blank wall with the concealer and cover-up being your 'fillers'. The eyeshadow, blusher and lipstick will create light and shade, and the balance and intensity of how you apply each one will make a difference to how the shape of your face and features appear.

How do you know your face shape?

• Look in the mirror and pull back all your hair from your face.
• Do not wear any clothing that clutters up your neckline. So a towel wrapped round you is best.
• Use a lipstick, crayon or something that is easily wiped from the mirror. Standing very close up to the mirror, draw the outline of your face on the mirror in front of you.
• Also be honest and critical with yourself to decide if you have any other prominent features such as a high forehead, long nose or receding chin.
• Once you have accepted your features you can disguise and balance them with your make-up and hairstyle.
• See pages 46-47 for the different face shapes.

Eyebrows

 Do you know how to shape your brows?

Before you start your make-up you need to look closely at your eyebrows. When did you last consider what they looked like? Have you plucked them recently or did you over pluck them years ago? What shape are they? Could they be improved? Or don't you care as you think they don't make a difference?

Plucking your eyebrows will open up your eyes and take ten years off your face. Eyebrows frame your eyes. Your eyes are the first thing that most people notice and are the 'front door' to your 'visible' emotions. So it is very important that your eyebrows are well groomed and plucked to work best for your face and eye shape. Your eyebrow shape can make your eyes appear more open, seem larger or smaller and completely change your facial look. If you look at many celebrity eyebrows, you will find that as the celebrities have become more high profile and groomed, all have undergone an eyebrow makeover from heavy thick brows to finer, groomed and contoured brows (think Liz Hurley from before wearing that life changing 'safety pin' red carpet dress to how she looks now).

I don't know where to start plucking from.

Your eyebrow shape will define your eyes. They should be gently arched and taper away. To find out exactly where the brows should start and end, you should hold a pencil or make-up brush vertically alongside your nose. Your inside brow edge should start at the point where the pencil meets it. The brow arch should be somewhere directly above your iris. The outer brow edge should ideally be at the point where your pencil creates an angled line from your nose past the edge of your eye to your brow edge. You should never pluck from above your eyebrows. Only pluck from beneath (in bright light so you can see what you're doing), tweezing a hair at a time, whilst checking in the mirror how this step by step removal is altering your brow shape. You don't want to end up with pencil-thin brows or rounded brows. To help you see the shape you would like to achieve, brush your eyebrows upwards into the shape you would like them to be, and then pencil in the shape you want. That way you can see where to pluck and not to pluck.

It hurts.

It's best to pluck after a warm shower or bath as your pores will be open. Always pull in the direction the hairs are growing.

Can I use any other method?

You can go to a salon to have your eyebrows shaped by threading. This is where hairs are removed one at a time with a tiny thread. You can also have them waxed. There are brow-shaping stencil kits you can buy that can help you make sure that your brow shape ends up being one that you wanted.

What shape is good for my face shape?

If you have close set eyes and you want to make them appear further apart, then lightly extend the brows further outward.

Eyes with a deep socket can take eyebrows that are slightly thicker. Eyes with only a little space between eye and brow need as much space as possible to open them up.

My face shape is oval.

Try to pluck them so they taper and slant upwards towards the temples. Take the most hairs away from underneath the outer edges.

My face shape is square.

Your eyebrow shape should soften your wide face shape with a gentle arched shape. As you have a strong face shape, you can take heavier eyebrows, so don't over pluck.

My face shape is rectangular.

As you want to widen your long face you want to keep your eyebrows strong but well-shaped, balancing out your square jawline.

My face shape is an inverted triangle.

As your face shape is wide on the forehead with high cheekbones, you want to have gently arched eyebrows which do not appear to make your upper face even wider. So keep them well-groomed and well plucked. Only the stronger face shapes can take heavier eyebrows.

My face shape is round.

You want to balance the roundness of your face with straighter lines. So when you pluck your eyebrows try to make them less curved tapering away to a slim line at the outer edges.

TIPS

Best tweezers

A good gripping pair of tweezers is essential to remove those stray brow hairs. The best used by most celebrity make-up artists and myself are by Tweezerman.

I have over plucked over the years and they won't grow back.

Once you have over plucked, especially over many years, you can't turn the clock back but you can try to do some repair work. With over-plucked eyebrows you will need to fill in where you would like the thicker eyebrow to be. You can use a natural shade of powder shadow with a chisel shaped brush or an eyebrow pencil. It is easiest to create a natural looking brow with a brush and powder with little feathery brush strokes, but pencil may last longer.

There is nothing you can do to make hairs grow back, but if you want to do something permanently instead of using make-up, you can have eyebrows tattooed. You don't visit a tattoo parlour but a semi-permanent make-up artist or salon where they specialise in semi-permanent make-up procedures. The missing eyebrows are tattooed on in feathery strokes. This will last around 18 months.

The eyebrows must be made to look natural – not too dark or 'one-line'.

How can I keep my eyebrows tamed? They always look unruly.

You can brush them into shape with an old, clean tooth brush or cleaned up mascara brush. Once brushed into shape you can use a clear mascara or brow gel to set them. If there is a stray, longer one you could trim it with nail scissors.

My eyebrows look so blonde they disappear.

You could tint your brows with a light brown eyelash tint. You can do this at home or at a beauty salon. This works very well and lasts around 6 weeks. Or you could use a powder shadow or pencil to emphasise your brows.

There are plenty of tools and products you can get your hands on for taming those eyebrows.

• *An old toothbrush*

• *The Body Shop Brow and Eyelash Comb*

• *Cover Girl Natural Lash and Brow Mascara*

• *MAC Brow Set Clear Brow Mascara*

Eyebrow definers

• *Laura Mercier eyebrow pencils: for filling in the gaps and defining the shape. Celebrity fan: Madonna.*

• *MAC Eyeshadow in Omega: it's not specifically for the brows but this shade works brilliantly for blondes and people with medium skin/hair.*

Eyebrow kits

• *ModelCo Eyebrowz Designer Brow Kit: a complete kit to shape and groom your brows. Celebrity fans: Elle Macpherson and Victoria Beckham.*

• *MAC Brow Set*

• *Estee Lauder Artist's Brow Stylist Mobile Essentials kit*

Make-up

So now that your eyebrows have been groomed and shaped, you can start on your make-up.

Everyone looks better with some make-up, especially as you get older. I meet so many women who tell me that they have never worn any and don't know how to apply it.

Applying your daily make-up should be something that is as familiar to you as brushing your teeth. Once you've put it on, you should be able to forget about

it. It's not necessary to cake it on. Less is *always* more.

It should be applied lightly and not be noticeable, especially during the daytime. It should enhance and draw attention to your best features, and can be used to make small eyes bigger, close-set eyes further apart, thin lips fuller, cheeks more contoured, nose more chiselled, under-eye shadows concealed. It can help you look less tired, younger, fresher and certainly more groomed.

'I apply make-up sparingly and quickly. It's important to be natural. A face that's not overly made up looks younger.'

Catherine Deneuve

There is no point putting on your best outfit for work or for a party unless you 'finish'. The finish is about the make-up as much as a stylish bag and shoes.

Decide how much time you have before you start your make-up as that will dictate how far you can go with your chosen look. You may have five minutes before the school run or before you go to work, but an hour before a party. Never experiment with make-up before you are about to go out. Save this for an evening in when you can remove it again if it doesn't work!

Q: Why don't you wear make-up?

Why should I change the habits of a lifetime?
Because you are embarking on a step-by-step journey to discovering the 'new you'. You will never know if something works for you until you try.

I feel make-up is unnecessary.
Everyone needs *some* make-up. OK… maybe not *everyone*, but you will certainly look an even better version of yourself with some, even if you feel good without it. Any one of the following can make a difference: concealer, blusher, a single application of mascara, or a hint of lip gloss.

I may look silly.
You won't look silly if you apply less rather than more, and apply it correctly with colours that work for your skin tone and age, which we'll consider later. People will notice you look healthy and well. Not that you are wearing make-up.

I think that anything more than some mascara or lipstick is overkill.
Then just wear those. There are no rules of what make-up you should or shouldn't wear. You have to feel comfortable and still feel like 'you'.

I don't know what products to buy.
Start off with the basic ones. You don't have to go for the most expensive. Very often factories that produce for top end cosmetic companies manufacture for the high street brands as well. Start with mascara, neutral coloured eyeshadows, maybe in a lighter and a darker grey or a lighter and a darker brown, a foundation that suits your skin type, some lip gloss and some blusher. It's important to use good soft bristle brushes, not the token miniature ones that accompany the products. You can find the customer enquiries number or website address for each make-up brand that I have mentioned at the back of this book.

> *❝The eyebrow pencil and false eyelashes were essential; my mother (Judy Garland) didn't feel dressed without them.❞*
>
> **Lorna Luft**

I don't know how to apply it.
Make-up is about enhancing your best features and detracting from your worst. Make-up should not be noticeable or too heavy, unless you are a model in a fashion or beauty photography shoot. You can learn how to apply simple daily make-up from this book following my step-by-step instructions. It's not hard and once you have had some practice your make-up routine can be quick and easy. You will wonder how you lived without using it at all. More glamorous evening make-up will take longer to experiment with. But it's like riding a bicycle. Once you have mastered it, you will never forget.

My make-up has been the same for the last 20 years.
Foundation badly applied, thickly plastered or the the wrong colour (too dark or too pink) will add years on to you. Also lipstick that is too red or too vibrant whether pink or coral will do no favours for older women. In all cases less is more. The key words to good make-up application are blend, blend and blend.

TIPS

Make-up brushes

To apply make-up well you need proper brushes. Ideally, you need a selection. At least one for eyeshadow, but a few would be better so that you can have one for each colour you use. These should be quite flat and easy to manipulate around the eye contours. Brushes for powder blusher and powder should be soft and largish. The eye brow brush can be chisel shaped. I find that shape the easiest to use. Lip brushes are small and pointed. You can buy natural bristle brushes at art shops and many celebrity make-up artists now create their own ranges of make-up and brushes at high street prices.

My favourite brushes are MAC. The ones at The Body Shop are great too and have won lots of awards.

6*What's wrong with having lines around your eyes, anyway? I actually like them... if you want to look better, get a new hairdo and learn how to do your make-up properly.*9

Make-up artist Bobbi Brown

Q: **When did you last update your make-up bag?**

When I ask my clients to show me their make-up bags, many show me ones with contents well past their sell-by date that have been languishing at the bottom of the bag since they started wearing make-up: lipsticks with no lipstick left in the barrel, colours that no longer suit their skin tones or hair colouring, tired 'free with the product' mini-brushes and sponge applicators, dried up gunky mascaras. It's important to update your make-up regularly.

Why do I need to update my make-up, I hardly ever wear it?
Most beauty products only have a shelflife of around six months. You may notice that your lipsticks and foundations begin to smell stale after too many months.

As you age, your skin tones change along with your hair colour and you will find that those products that you have had forever no longer suit you. You may also need to change your make-up style to be appropriate to your age. (We'll talk more about this later.)

'You wouldn't recognise me from photographs 20 years ago. I feel you change every 12 years.'
Francesca Annis

Q: **Do you know how to adapt your make-up to your age?**

Are you stuck in a make-up time warp? More mature skins with wrinkles and crow's feet need foundations that have light reflective qualities. Matte eyeshadows are better than shiny and anything glittery or pearlised is really not very flattering for more mature skin.

Q: **Do you have no time in the morning to put on any make-up?**

Everyone can use a little help, however beautiful they are, and how long can it take to put on a little mascara and some lip gloss? You need to find a make-up routine that suits your daily routine.

'The director may tell me it looks perfect, but I always find that stray hair or eyebrow. I can't wait for my looks to fade.'

Jennifer Lopez

I'm always late!
Maybe you don't want to wear a foundation but you could try a tinted moisturiser, which will moisturise and give you a healthy glow. It only takes a few minutes to apply and is two products in one application, saving time! Instead of wearing mascara, have you considered dyeing your eyelashes? It saves you having to put mascara on each day.

I have to get the children ready for school.
Blusher always helps you look healthier and gives your cheeks some shape whilst lip gloss adds that extra finishing touch. Why can't you feel good about yourself, even if you're on the school run? It may only take an extra five minutes in your getting up and out routine. If you're a newly single mum, you never know who you could meet outside the school gates… There may be some newly single dads out there too.

I have to leave too early for work.
If you deal with clients or customers face to face, how you look will be associated with a perception of the brand. So however smart your clothes may be, it is important to wear some make-up as it will make you look not only healthier but better groomed and more polished.

 Q: **How do you adapt your make-up to your face shape?**

(See 'How do you know your face shape' section on pages 48-49.)
How you apply your make-up will affect the look of your face shape. So you can use blusher, shading, highlights and eyeshadow to create contours and the impression of better balanced features. To highlight, you can use a 'highlighter' powder, cream or pencil that is similar to a neutral, pale, shiny eyeshadow or a light reflective product such as the Yves Saint Laurent Touche Eclat concealing and highlighting brush pen.

I have a round face.

Use light and shade to create contours. Apply your blusher onto the apples of your cheeks (the fleshy front area) keeping the colour inwards rather than outwards.

I have a narrow face.

Use blusher to draw the eye outwards, applying the blusher less centrally, more toward the cheekbones.

I have a square face.

Use light and shade as you would with a round face shape. Apply the blusher to the apples of the cheeks.

I have a double chin.

Use a browny shade of blusher subtly under the jawline. Make sure there are no tide marks. This will draw the attention away from your chin. Blusher and highlighter will attract attention to the eye area and the cheekbones.

I have a wide nose.

You can shade down either side of the nose with a browny shade of blusher. Be minimal – you don't want to look as though you have bruises.

I have a long nose.

You can shade under the tip of the nose and highlight down the centre.

I have close set eyes.

Take your eyeshadow shading further out than usual. Use a lighter shade of shadow on the inner part of your lid whilst the darker shade and shading should be toward the outer edge.

Eyeliner can start from the centre of your eyelash line on your upper lid to slightly outside your eye edge.

I have wide set eyes.

Apply your eye-shadow colour more centrally and in a more rounded way on your eyelid and into the socket, rather than taking the colour outwards. You can use your paler shadow on the central part of the lid, with the deeper shade into the whole socket – not just the outer edge. You can take the eyeliner all the way along the eyelash line on the top lid from the inside corner, but stopping the line short at the outer edge.

I have small eyes.

Never use liner on the upper lid, or a dark shadow as an under-eyeliner as they will close up your eye. Use a darker shadow in the socket to lengthen outwards, and from the mid to outer eyelash edge to lengthen outwards, with lots of mascara mostly on the upper outer lashes.

I have a high forehead.

Use a matte powder bronzer or a brownish toned blusher horizontally along the top of your forehead. The shading will help create an impression of a lower forehead.

I have a wide forehead.

Use the matte bronzer powder or brownish toned blusher vertically down the temples, to help give the appearance of a narrower forehead. The shading will again create this impression.

I would like Kate Moss style cheekbones.
Use your blusher not only on the apples of your cheeks but in a more lengthy and diagonal way.

I always look shiny even if I keep powdering.
Try using a product to stop greasiness before you apply your make-up.

Oil absorbers

Used under your foundation or make-up, to inhibit shine and greasiness.

• *Elemis Daily Shine Control: this moisturiser with jasmine and rose helps minimise shine and keeps the face looking matte whilst moisturising and also helps prevent spots.*

• *Caudalie Vinopure Matte Finish Fluid. This helps regulate oil with antioxidant plant extracts.*

'I'm not interested in age. People who tell me their age are silly. You're as old as you feel.'
Elizabeth Arden

Sometimes my skin looks tired whatever moisturiser I use.
You can try a primer or illuminator, before you apply your make-up and after your moisturiser.

Primer

These help even out skin tones, create a smooth surface for foundation and give a radiant glow. A primer is not a moisturiser but for use between moisturising and applying make-up.

• *Laura Mercier Foundation Primer Oil Free. Celebrity fan: Kate Hudson.*

• *NARS Make-up Primer: this is a dual-ended concealer/primer duo for under the eyes and anywhere else on the face.*

Illuminator

These will give you an instantly fresher look.

• *Clarins Beauty Flash Balm: an instant lift and illuminator.*

• *Pout After glow: illuminator to leave skin looking hydrated and fresh. Celebrity fan: Gwyneth Paltrow.*

• *Olay Complete Care Multi-radiance with SPF 15: you can use this on its own, under your foundation or mixed with it to give a glowing finish. It smells good too.*

Foundation

The most important element of your make-up is foundation which serves to even out your skin tones, allowing the rest of your make-up to create highlights and shadows. Foundation should be applied to be invisible. It should match your skin tone and even out any irregularities of colouration, pigmentation and blemishes. It should be applied with your fingertips or a small make-up sponge to achieve even coverage. When applying your foundation, always make sure that it is blended out at the jawline and the neck.

Never ever try foundation colours on the back of your hand. The correct place is at the bottom of your cheek near your jawline. This is where your foundation should blend and match your skin tone. You will not be able to see the true colour of the foundation unless you take yourself and a mirror into the daylight as the lighting in department stores can be misleading.

TIPS

Triangular sponges

These small make-up sponges are used to apply foundation more subtly, smoothly and evenly. They can be dampened before use to lessen make-up 'tide marks' and caked make-up. You can buy them in most high street chemists.

Light-reflecting foundations

You can help diminish the look of fine lines and wrinkles with light-reflecting foundations.

• *L'Oreal Translucide Healthy Glow make-up*

• *Superdrug GOSH X-ceptional Wear long-lasting light-reflecting make-up*

• *Chantecaille Future Skin Oil Free Gel Foundation: it's very lightweight and light-reflective, with natural ingredients such as aloe, camomile and arnica to soothe sensitive skin. Celebrity fans: Kate Blanchett, Cameron Diaz and Kate Hudson.*

• *Jane Iredale Liquid Minerals Foundation: this natural foundation is my daily favourite and makes your skin look glowing, un-made up yet still gives coverage.*

My skin feels dry when I wear foundation.

If your skin feels too dry when you wear foundation you could try adding a touch of your daily moisturiser when you apply it. Or you can choose a foundation that has extra hydrating properties.

'Extra help' foundations

• *Prescriptives Luxe Soft Glow Moisture Make-up*

• *Lancôme Photogenic Ultra Confort Light-reflecting Moisturising Make-up with SPF 12: this foundation is excellent for dry and occasionally dry skin as it is enriched with a combination of oils, hydrating ingredients and vitamin C, ginseng and ginkgo to help keep the skin moist and supple. The light-reflective quality helps give flawless healthy looking skin whilst the blue pigments take away grey from dull complexions. Celebrity fan: Drew Barrymore.*

• *Clinique Dewy Smooth Anti-aging Make-up: this is a line-minimising, light-reflecting foundation with extra moisturising properties.*

• *Estee Lauder Re-Nutriv Ultimate Lifting Crème make-up SPF 15: this is a cream make-up that helps to boost moisture levels to create a smoother more radiant complexion. After eight weeks of use it helps lift and tone the skin, reducing the appearance of fine lines and wrinkles. Celebrity fans: Elizabeth Hurley and Gwyneth Paltrow.*

• *La Prairie Skin Caviar Concealer Foundation: this is a foundation that creates a flawless skin with amazing coverage. It also has a colour match concealer in the lid.*

• *RVB Lift Effect Creamy Foundation: contains a formula to soften the facial lines and help prevent wrinkles.*

My make-up always settles into my surrounding eye wrinkles.

Buy a foundation that is advertised to be suited to more mature skins and that is also light reflective. Don't use a heavy foundation and powder, especially around the eye area. Blend it away before you reach the surrounding eye lines. Be minimal with face powder as it tends to sit in the wrinkles. Keep to only powdering the T-zone of forehead and nose and chin or you could try blotting papers instead of powder (see powders and blotting papers).

Spray foundation

This foundation can be applied with your fingertips or by spraying for an even natural look.

• *Dior Diorskin Airflash Mist Make-up: this is a great product and once you have got used to spraying on your foundation with even movements, it looks great on the skin. Celebrity make-up artists love it.*

Foundation that gives a finish with more coverage

• *MAC Studio Fix Fluid SPF 15: although this has great coverage, it doesn't make you look too made up. This is the make-up often used on celebrity photo shoots.*

But I really don't like the feeling of make-up on my skin.

Make-up should not feel heavy on the skin and certainly not look as if it is caked on. If you wear a foundation, it should not be visible but only be there to even out your complexion. Most of the foundations I've mentioned are so light that you can still have coverage without looking like you are wearing any. But if you really feel adamant about this then you could try a tinted moisturiser.

I have facial hair and when I wear foundation it emphasises the hairs.

Just as a wall needs smoothing, sanding and preparing before painting, so does your face before you apply make-up. If you have superfluous facial hair, either on the lips or at the sides of your face, it is important to remove it. Especially as you reach the menopause, as you may find odd hairs sprouting up where there weren't ones before.

If you bleach your facial hair, it will become less noticeable, but when you add foundation, the make-up will sit on the hairs, making them more visible. You should look into laser removal or electrolysis to help decrease your hair. Laser, although much more expensive, is quicker and less painful (see non-surgical procedures). Never, ever shave. You will end up with bristles like a man (see section on hair removal).

Tinted moisturiser

These moisturisers can be used instead of foundation as they will still give some cover whilst also giving a healthy glow.

• *Benefit You Rebel SPF 15 tinted moisturiser*

• *DuWop Revolution Face Perfect Skin Above the Chin: this tinted moisturiser is used in Hollywood make-up rooms as it leaves the skin looking sexy and glowing whilst still covering up any imperfections.*

• *Laura Mercier Tinted Moisturiser SPF 20 Oil Free*

• *Dr Haushka Translucent Bronze Concentrate: this holistic delicious smelling make-up works in balance with the skin and gives a great golden glow. Celebrity fans: Melanie Sykes, Jade Jagger.*

• *Dr NV Perricone MD Active Tinted Moisturiser SPF 15: contains ingredients to help tone skin and minimise fine lines.*

Bronzers

I would like to look browner.

Foundation should not make you appear suntanned or darker. That is the job of a bronzing powder.

• *Guerlain Terracotta Moisturising Bronzing Powder: with a dusting of this classic bronzing powder* you can look natural and healthy throughout the year. It comes in two shades for pale blondes and olive-skinned brunettes. Celebrity fans: Kylie Minogue, Claudia Schiffer, Cat Deeley.

• Dr Haushka Bronzing Powder

• Dior Bronze Essential Bronzing Powder in light tan: a subtle bronzing powder to give a golden glow. This powder works better used straight after a moisturiser or tinted moisturiser for a deeper colour.

• Chanel Irréelle Soleil Silky Bronzing Powder in colour 25 Savannah: this bronzing powder gives a subtle golden glow and is great for using both on the face and the décolleté.

Self tan for the face

I would like a more permanent facial tan.
A fake tan for the face needs to be applied evenly as it does not wash off. It fades gradually.

• Clarins Radiance-plus Self-tanning Cream Gel for the face: great for fair complexions for a natural tanned appearance.

• Clarins Sheer Bronze Self-tanning Hydrating Gel: this not only tans within two hours but also moisturises.

Concealer

I have dark under-eye shadows. If I cover them with foundation then I look even more crinkly around the eyes.
Use a concealer, not your foundation base, to freshen and rejuvenate skins and lighten any under-eye dark shadows or lines, and nose to mouth lines. Apply with a brush, and blend it away with light tapping movements with your finger.

These concealers are a key product to have in your make-up bag. They contain light-reflective properties that help disguise dark eye shadows and lines. You apply them after you have put on your foundation. This is the product that will make you look instantly younger and refreshed.

• Laura Mercier Undercover: this is oilier than Laura Mercier's Secret Camouflage (see camouflage products). It is better to glide onto the skin and not cake under the eye.

• Yves Saint Laurent Touche Eclat concealer pen: this light-reflecting concealer is in nearly every celebrity's make-up bag that I have worked with. You can use the Yves Saint Laurent Lisse Expert Eye and Lip Anti-wrinkle Concentrate underneath it for maximum effect.

• Dior Skinflash Radiance Booster Pen

• *Stila Eye Concealer*

• *NARS Eye Brightener*

• *Prescriptives Invisible Line Smoother*

• *Clinique Line Smoothing Concealer*

• *Asda Skin Expert Crow's Feet Diminisher*

• *The Body Shop Lightening Touch*

My age spots and blemishes still show under my foundation.
You can't hide blemishes or age spots with your foundation as you'll end up with a caked mask. So try using a warm-toned concealer or spot cover, applied with a small brush onto the small problem areas after applying your foundation.

Spot cover up

This is for specifically targeting and covering blemishes. One shade paler than your skin is best. You can apply these before or after your foundation. But I find that application after foundation is better, as you can then blend away the cover up more effectively .

• *Benefit Galactic Shield! concealer. Celebrity fans: Kiera Knightley, Britney Spears.*

• *MAC Select Moisturecover*

Camouflage make-up

This make-up is designed for extra coverage.

• *Cover FX Total Coverage cream foundations and setting powders: this brand was designed to conceal acne, vitiligo, rosacea and burns but it can be used simply to create a flawless complexion. Celebrity fans: Cate Blanchett and Angelina Jolie.*

• *Estee Lauder Maximum Cover Camouflage Make-up SPF 15*

• *Laura Mercier Secret Camouflage: for blemishes anywhere on the face. It's in two colours for mixing and blending. Celebrity fans: Sarah Jessica Parker, Madonna.*

• *Estee Lauder Maximum Cover Lightweight Make-up: great for covering blemished skin in the sun and also waterproof.*

Blusher

So how do I know which blusher to use? I don't know whether to use powder or cream blusher.
Cream blusher can be applied with your fingertips or a medium-sized flat brush, but it is more difficult to apply than a powder blusher, as the edges of the blusher area must be blended away. Powder blusher is applied with a larger soft brush with small circular

motions. Cream blusher will give your cheeks more of a glow, whilst powder blusher colour will give more depth of colour.

I don't know where to put the blusher.

Look in the mirror and smile whilst applying the blusher to the apple of your cheeks. Blusher should be subtly applied to the apples of the cheeks, not below (the apples being the fleshy front area of your cheeks, not your cheekbones). You never want your cheek colour to be a *noticeable* daub. It should just be giving you a healthier, rosier hue. You don't want to look like Coco the clown. If you have any spots in the area where you may be placing the blusher, apply powder over the concealer before you apply the blusher, unless you are using a cream blusher.

Blusher (cream)

• *MAC Cheekhue*

• *Pout Flush Blush, Fuschia Fusion shade: an easy to blend cream blush to give you that healthy glow. Celebrity fan: Scarlett Johansson.*

Blusher (mousse)

• *Guerlain Divinora Bubble Blush: this is long lasting as it's a mousse and feels wonderfully light. It should be applied with your fingertip and* then blended away. It looks natural and fresh. You can wear it over your moisturiser or your foundation.

Lip and cheek stain

• *Vincent Longo Lip and Cheek Gel*

• *Benefit Benetint Rose-coloured Cheek and Lip Tint: you apply a couple of drops of the stain on to the apples of the cheeks and blend quickly in.*

Blusher (powder)

• *MAC Powder Blush: in all shades but Pink Swoon is really good.*

• *NARS Blush in Orgasm shade. Celebrity fans: Catherine Zeta Jones, Kirsten Dunst.*

• *Bourjois Blush: the first brand to bring out the small round pots of powder blush in a huge range of colours. My favourite pinky blushes are 48 Cendre de Roses and 35 Lune D'Or.*

Highlighter

Highlighter will highlight the area you put it. So if you wish to accentuate your cheekbones or brow bones this is the product for you.

• *NARS The Multiple in Maldives shade: a highlighter for cheeks, eyes and lips. Celebrity fans: Catherine Zeta Jones, Gwyneth Paltrow.*

Eyeshadow

Eyeshadow should be applied with a good, soft, natural, long-handled paintbrush style brush, and always be blended away, leaving no hard lines. It is impossible to achieve this with the free sponge applicators that come with the eyeshadows. Using light and shade, eyeshadow can be used to change the appearance of your eye shape (see make-up for your face shape).

My eyeshadow never stays put, but slides into the creases.
The trick is to put foundation over the eyelids first, then apply the powder eyeshadow.

My lids are now droopy with no defined socket.
With droopy eyelids it is very important not to let the eye-shadow sink into the skin folds. Gently lift each eyebrow with your finger, so that you can see the socket area more clearly and make it easier to apply the shadow. Keep the colour on the lid paler and darker in the socket, to give the illusion of a still existing socket definition.

MAC eyeshadows are great. They have an amazing array of colours, are fantastic to apply and stay on brilliantly. MAC is my own choice of eyeshadow and that of many celebrities and celebrity make-up artists.

I would like to wear my eyeshadow when I am on the beach.

- *Lancôme Color Dose Eyes: a waterproof cream eye colour.*
- *Superdrug GOSH waterproof eyeshadow in 'Love that brown' shade*

Eyeliner pencils/kohl

To add extra intensity to your eye make-up and definition you can use eyeliners or kohl.

Eyeliner pencils are nice and soft, don't drag on the eye, and last well. You can use them along the upper lid lash line, or inside the bottom lid edge. Kohl can be used in the same way as it usually comes in pencil form too. It can have a softer and smudgier effect than eye pencils. If you want a natural effect that accentuates the eye, then use a brown or black. If you want to follow a seasonal fashion trend, then you can use colour such as blue or green or a metallic.

* *Shu Uemura Drawing Pencil: these are available in matte and metallic finishes that glide easily onto the eyelid and don't smudge. They are waterproof and long lasting.*

* *Estee Lauder Artist's Eye Pencil in soft smudge brown*

* *Prescriptives Softlining Pencil*

* *Lancôme Le crayon Kohl: this soft eyeliner pencil can be used on the top lash line and inside the lower eyelid. Celebrity fan: Keira Knightley.*

* *MAC Eye Kohl Pencil in Smoulder*

Liquid eyeliner

You may prefer liquid liner, as it can give a more defined line than the smudgy or softer effect of pencils or Kohl pencils.

Use black or colour for enhancing the lash line.

* *Urban Decay Liquid Liner. Celebrity fans: Angelina Jolie, Gwen Stefani.*

I would like my liner and kohl to be waterproof.

* *Dior Eyeliner Waterproof, in seaside blue*

* *MAC Liquidlast eyeliner*

* *Superdrug GOSH Waterproof Eyeliner*

* *Jemma Kidd Define Stay Put Eyeliner: a water and smudge proof eyeliner. Celebrity fan: Kate Moss.*

* *Lancôme Le Crayon Kohl Waterproof*

Eyelashes

Eyelash curlers

Use eyelash curlers before you apply your mascara or false lashes. You can also buy heated eyelash curlers . These can be more effective instantly, in the same way as heated rollers or curling tongs are when creating a curly hair style. Eyelash curlers open up your eyes and make your lashes look so much longer.

- *Shu Uemura eyelash curlers: these are many make-up artists' first choice of curlers.*

- *The Body Shop eyelash curlers*

- *Ruby and Millie Eyelash Kit heated eyelash curlers*

Mascara

Apply your mascara from under the base of the lashes to the tips. Start at the centre of the lashes, then work to the inner and outer edge (or whichever way is comfortable for you). Then repeat the application from above the lashes. When you apply the mascara to the bottom lashes, make sure you don't get the mascara onto your skin. If you do make a mistake, remove the spot with a cotton bud. It's easier to put mascara on the top lashes when you raise your chin and look down the tip of your nose: it helps stop your newly wet lashes brushing your lids.

If you are short sighted, and you don't wear contact lenses, but do wear specs, you may find it easier to apply your makeup in a magnifying mirror, or to buy specs that have lenses that fold down individually for ease of make-up application.

Mascara gives the finishing touch to your eye make-up. You can add less or more according to whether you are going for a natural daytime or full on party make-up.

Mascara should not be gunky, heavy or cloggy when applied, especially when it is for daytime wear. Brown mascara can often be more flattering than black if you are fair-haired and fair-skinned. Mascara comes in all types now, from just adding colour to those that add volume.

- *Max Factor 2000 Calorie Dramatic Look: a good mascara for daily use.*

- *Lancome Hypnose Custom-wear Volume Mascara: you can keep building up the volume without caking or clogging. Celebrity fans: Kate Hudson, Mena Suvari, Drew Barrymore.*

- *Dior Diorshow Mascara Backstage Make-up: this mascara has a chunky brush that is great for applying masses of mascara quickly.*

- *Clinique High Definition Lashes: a good mascara for those with sensitive eyes.*

- *L'Oreal Volume Shocking two step mascara: for big lashes!*

- *Estee Lauder Illusionist Maximum Curling Mascara: gives big lashes without weight and clogging.*

Cotton buds

These are great for cleaning up those accidental smudges of mascara, and tidying up hard eyeshadow edges which should always be blended away.

My mascara always ends up smudged around my eyes.
You could try a good waterproof mascara, even if you aren't on the beach. If you are at a party, getting hot and sweaty, there is nothing worse than having mascara running down your cheeks.

• *Max Factor Lash Lift Waterproof*

• *Bourjois Maxifrange Waterproof Mascara in Vert Honolulu: a lash lengthening waterproof mascara in a dark green.*

• *Yves Saint Laurent Mascara Aquaresistant*

• *Jemma Kidd Make-up School Lasting Tint: a semi-permanent waterproof mascara that lasts for three days. Celebrity fan: Teri Hatcher.*

But I don't like the feel of mascara.
Why not try having your eyelashes tinted, if you don't like wearing mascara? You can also do this yourself at home. If you want to wake up looking as glamorous as you did the night before, there is also the option of lash extensions that can be applied professionally at salons. These will last for a few months.

• *Home eyelash tint: Eyelure Dylash lash tint*

False Lashes

How do I apply false lashes?
Begin by curling your own eyelashes with your eyelash curlers. Put a tiny bit of glue along the band of the eyelashes. False eyelashes with a clear band may look better on than those with a black band, especially if you are a novice eyelash applier. This is because the base of the false lashes is less visible, so any imperfections that occur during application will be less visible. Leave the glue to dry until it's tacky rather than wet. Using tweezers, place the eyelashes on the eyeline. Do not leave a gap. You can use a liquid eyeliner after you have stuck on the lashes. It can cover up any mistakes. Finish off with a coat of mascara which is the key to blending your fake and natural lashes together.

• *Shu Uemura False lashes: you can choose from very thick and long to more subtle.*

TIPS

Vaseline

This can be used on eyelashes, brows and lips. This not only nourishes your lashes, but gives them a glossy natural look. It helps set your eyebrows. It moisturises your lips.

Lips

Lip liners

Lip liner should not show. If you do use it, it should be the same tone as your own lips, used to re-shape the lip line, ready for infill by lipstick or lip gloss.

- *Jemma Kidd Make-up School Lip Line Duo: these pencils have a neutral colour one end and a choice of five shades to blend into your chosen lipstick/gloss colour at the other end.*

- *MAC Spice Lip Liner: the choice of many celebrity make-up artists. Celebrity fan: Linda Evangelista.*

My lipstick always bleeds into the lines around my lips.

To stop your lipstick bleeding into those feather lines around the lip line, set the lipstick colour. Put a tissue between your lips and gently close them onto the freshly applied lipstick to soak up the excess.

Or you can use this clever product:

- *DuWop Reverse Lip Liner: this lip liner is applied just outside the lips and stops lipstick feathering and bleeding. Celebrity fan: Scarlett Johansson.*

Lipstick

Lipsticks come both matte (not shiny) and glossy.

- *Guerlain KissKiss Lipstick: a moisturising (with vitamins A and E), long-lasting (up to five hours), delicious smelling lipstick. There are a huge variety of shades in matte or pearl. The Guerlain lipstick is a luxurious classic. It looks and feels wonderfully elegant to use.*

- *Lancôme Juicy Tubes: this lip gloss is the celebrity favourite, as it's so glossy and lasts well. Celebrity*

fans: Sienna Miller, Kate Hudson, Angelina Jolie, Jennifer Lopez, Victoria Beckham.

• Pout Lip Gloss Light My Fire in Smouldering Hot Coral shade. Celebrity fans: Beyoncé Knowles and Kylie Minogue.

• Jeff +Maggie Lip Gloss: available at selected Matalan stores. Great quality and colour for a high street brand.

• Estee Lauder Double Wear Stay-in-place Lip Duo: a long-lasting moisturising lip colour duo.

• Chanel Rouge Allure Luminous Satin Lip Colour: a great classic lipstick. The best red colour for pink-toned skins is 09 Lover and for yellow-toned, sallow skins is 08 Brilliant.

• DuWop Lip Venom: this lip gloss delivers bee-stung lips! You can wear it alone or over lip colour. Celebrity fans: Gwen Stefani, Naomi Watts, Paris Hilton, Britney Spears, Cindy Crawford, Eva Longoria.

• Sovage Instant Lip Plumper: this US product tingles on application (giving the extra plump) and tastes and smells delicious, with a slight aroma of cocoa butter.

Lip gloss and lip plump

If you wish to be more subtle about your make-up then lip gloss may be more appropriate for you than lipstick. Lip gloss is easier to apply, as it can be applied with less precision.

You can also give your lips a little 'plump' at the same time as adding the colour.

• Benefit Color Plump! This comes in three colours. It's a plumping lip colour pencil with a lipstick finish.

• Pout Plump: best-selling plumping lip gloss, to give you that fuller pout. Celebrity fan: Scarlett Johansson.

Powder

Should you powder your face?

A light dusting of powder can be used to fix make-up straight after application (with a large soft brush or velvety powder puff pad) or to blot away shine later in the day. It should not be used liberally. Less is always more, especially around the eyes as powder can sit in your wrinkles if over-zealously applied.

- *Chantecaille loose powder talc, oil and lanolin free: it feels very light on the skin. Celebrity fans: Charlize Theron; Goldie Hawn, Jennifer Aniston.*

I always look shiny after an hour or so.

Always carry a pack of blotting papers with you. They are a great way to remove excess shine as they will blot the greasy areas instead of creating a build up of powder.

- *Shu Uemura Face Paper*
- *MAC Blot Film*
- *Superdrug Clarity Shine Control Paper*

Q: Do you know how to transform your daytime make-up into night-time make-up?

I work late and have to go out for the evening straight from work.

With no time to wash your face before going out, you can re-moisturise (especially around the eye area); touch up your concealer to hide your under eye shadows, and re-apply your blusher. You can add to your eyeshadow and re-apply your eyeliner. You can go much darker for the evening. Add masses of mascara and finally lip gloss. This should take no more than five minutes.

I don't know how to make my everyday make-up more glamorous for a party.

An evening make-up can be darker and smokier around the eyes and have a stronger coloured lipstick than day time, but it is best to *either* have dark smokey eyes and natural coloured lips *or* strong coloured lips and natural eyes. Never the two as you will look over made up. There is a fine line between over made up and a sexy glamorous make-up.

> **Beauty is not an easy thing to live with. Often the most beautiful people are the most self-conscious.**
>
> Sarah Doukas, Storm modelling agency

When it comes to make-up, my message is, be yourself and let yourself be seen. Don't slosh so much make-up on that you can't see the real person.

Julie Andrews

Eyecare

Looking after your eyes is not only about your skincare and the make-up around them but also the eyes themselves.

Wear sunglasses to protect your eyes from the sun's UV rays and wear glasses or contact lenses so that you can see properly. You would be surprised to know how many people I meet who go round in a constant blur. It is also important to have regular eye check-ups at your optician's.

Glasses

If you wear glasses, make them part of your wardrobe. Glasses can be an attractive fashion accessory that enhances your personality, colouring and face shape, not something to pretend you aren't wearing. Don't buy a pair that you will only wear in private or that are invisible on your face. You could choose ones that make a statement about your personality, just as your clothes do.

Q: **How can you choose the best spectacles for your face shape?**

(See 'How do you know your face shape' section on pages 48-49.)

Firstly, make sure that the spectacles sit correctly on the bridge of your nose. If your nose is long then wear the specs a little lower down and if your nose is short then you can wear them a little higher up. Your eyes must appear to be central in the lenses. If you are very short-sighted or long-sighted the optical prescription of the lenses may give your eyes a different appearance through the spectacles, so it is important to consult with your optician. But the most important thing is that they feel comfortable and give you good vision. Determine your face shape so that you can choose the best specs. It's all about complementing and balancing your features.

My face shape is oval.

You can wear any shape spectacles. But take your nose shape into consideration and make sure that your spectacle size is in proportion to your face.

My face shape is square.

Never echo your face shape with a square pair of spectacles but wear a softer more rounded or oval shape.

My face is rectangular with a square chin.

You must choose frames which are wide enough for your face shape but which do not echo your rectangular shaped face. You could wear really strong coloured and large frames which make a statement on your face.

My face is an inverted triangle shape, with a wide forehead and cheekbones with a small pointy chin.

You should wear frames which are not too wide and do not make your upper face appear wider still.

My face is round.

You should wear frames which are opposite to your face shape, so not round ones. Best for you are square or rectangular shapes that widen your face.

Q: Which colour glasses should you choose for your skin-colouring?

I have a pinky-toned complexion with fair-hair.

I have a yellow-toned complexion with fair hair.

Both complexion tones will be better with brown, tortoiseshell or lighter coloured frames as you have fair hair. Silver rims are better for pinky-tone skins and gold rims are better for yellow-toned skins.

I am dark skinned.

I have a pale complexion with dark hair.

You can wear strong coloured frames, even black.

Skincare

Your skin is the visual indication of how you have lived your life. Whether or not you are blessed with good genes, if you treat your skin well it will repay you years later by still looking great. If treated with anything less than respect and nurturing, it will be a reminder when you look in the mirror of how constant abuse can destroy a relationship!

Great skin needs you to maintain it in many ways. You can help hold back the ageing process with a healthy lifestyle, exercise, sleep, good nutrition and

> **There isn't any woman who doesn't look every day and minute of her age. We can't be, nor look, younger than we are, but we can be well preserved.**
>
> **Lillie Langtry**

drinking at least two litres of water a day. Sun exposure, alcohol and cigarettes are all detrimental.

Careful skincare and minimum exposure to direct sun are the most important things to do to maintain a beautiful complexion. You need to exfoliate, cleanse and moisturise. Toning is less important.

A skincare regime should take no longer than five or ten minutes and once you have a routine it is part of your life. A beauty closet does not need to consist of lots of products. Just basic ones that you use twice a day.

Exfoliate

Exfoliation helps to lift dead skin cells and encourage your skin to regenerate before moisturising.

• *Biotherm Biosource Clarifying Exfoliating Gel*

• *Dermalogica Daily Microfoliant. Celebrity fan: Erin O' Connor.*

Cleanse

'Cleansing is all important. It keeps the skin supple.'

Julie Andrews

Facial cleansers come in all sorts of guises from oil, to cream, to foaming, to pads. To keep your skin looking its best, you should cleanse first thing in the morning and last thing at night and always remove your make-up before going to sleep (however tired you are). The type of cleanser you use is as much about personal choice as your skin type. Some of you may prefer a cleansing milk. Others may prefer an oil and others may like a foaming wash. Although cleansing pads or wipes are convenient for your overnight bag or holidays, they are not as efficient as proper cleansers.

Can I just use soap and water?
Never use an ordinary hand soap to wash your face. It will be too drying.

Cleansers

• *She Uemura Cleansing Balancing Beauty Oil Premium A/O: this cleansing oil is extra gentle, great for combating the signs of ageing and contains the antioxidant green tea and natural plant extracts.*

• *Laura Mercier Purifying Oil, Light: it cleanses without drying the skin.*

• *Clinique Anti-Blemish Solutions Cleansing Foam*

• *SK-11 Facial Clear Solution*

• *Eve Lom Cleanser: a waxy pomade removed with a muslin cloth and water that will transform the condition of your skin, used only once daily at night-time. Celebrity fans: Laura Bailey, Sophie Dahl, Uma Thurman, Lauren Bacall, Meg Ryan, Julianne Moore.*

• *Liz Earle Cleanse & Polish Hot Cloth Cleanser: a gentle natural cleanser to use with warm water and a cloth. This is similar in style to the Eve Lom cleanser.*

• *Elemis Rehydrating Rosepetal Cleanser: rose is great for mature and dry/dehydrated skins. This cleanser moisturises too and can also help diminish the redness of broken capillaries.*

• *Superdrug Simply Pure Calming Cleanser*

• *Skin Wisdom Deep Cleansing Balm by Bharti Vyas for Tesco*

• *Nivea Visage Facial Cleansing Wipes: these deep cleanse without irritation. They are handy for travel and keeping in your make up bag.*

Eye make-up remover

A cleanser may not always do the combined job of face cleanser and an eye make-up remover.

• *Kiehl's Supremely Gentle Eye Make-up Remover: this is great for sensitive eyes and perfect for contact lens wearers. It not only cleanses gently whilst moisturising, but also contains soothing and antioxidant ingredients.*

I never bother to take off my make-up before going to bed.
You must always take off your make-up before going to bed. Otherwise it will soak into your pores and your skin will never get a chance to breathe properly.

When you've finished your routine of cleansing, splash your face with cold water. The colder the better, it wakes your skin up and helps circulation.

Moisturise

When should I moisturise?
Always after cleansing your face first thing in the morning (before applying your make-up) and last thing at night

before going to bed. After washing your face, pat in the moisturiser and wait five minutes, if you have time, for it to sink in before applying your make-up.

Should I buy a separate moisturiser for day and night?

Daytime moisturisers tend to be lighter than the night-time ones, which are richer and more nourishing. The more mature your skin, the more nourishing and richer the moisturiser you can take. If you use too rich a moisturiser when you are younger or have a tendency to an oily skin, you may find your skin becomes clogged and greasy.

How should I apply my moisturiser?

Use a gentle fingertip application with an upward motion so as not to drag the skin downwards. Tap or pat your moisturiser with your fourth fingertips (these exert the least pressure) into the sensitive eye area. Never drag or rub. Skincare is all about treating your skin gently. Massaging your face, when moisturising, is good for circulation. Increased blood flow will help regenerate skin cells.

I can't afford an expensive moisturiser.

The moisturiser doesn't have to be an expensive brand. Take a tip from the ageless Shakira Caine, Joan Collins or even Yasmin Le Bon who have all used and praised high street brands like Nivea, Olay, Vaseline and E45.

I love the Nivea products. I think they are fantastic value and are as good as many of the expensive brands.

Are there different moisturisers for your skin type?

There is something for everyone. All beauty products, from skincare to make-up, are specially formulated to suit your specific skin type. Some moisturisers will suit your skin better than others, whilst cleansers, toners and make-up removers are all formulated to work best for your skin type too. Even your foundation can 'work' for your skin (not just its colouring).

In addition to using the correct beauty products for your skin type, it is also important to drink two litres of water daily to hydrate your skin (and body) and have a healthy diet and exercise regularly.

The types of skin are:

Oily

Your skin is likely to be open-pored and often prone to appearing shiny not long after make-up application. But oily skin usually tans easily and ages better than dry skin, so you are the lucky ones. Mediterranean, sallow skins are usually oily. It is best to use oil-free products on this type of skin, as otherwise they can make an oily skin too greasy and become spotty.

Dry

Dry skins are often pale or freckly Celtic skins. Dry skins lap up moisturisers and need lots of care and attention, especially as they age less well than oily skins. Your beauty products should have extra hydrating and moisturising properties.

Combination (usually oily down the 'T-zone' and dry elsewhere)

The T-zone is the forehead, nose and either side of the nose and chin. You can mix and match your beauty products to suit your combination skin. As your skin ages, you may find that your combination skin becomes drier overall.

Mature

Mature skins can be oily or dry but will need richer, more hydrating products to nourish the skin, especially overnight.

Spotty or acne-prone

Even if you have problem skin you must still moisturise. Using a moisturiser will not create an oilier skin or more spots. If you cleanse and exfoliate regularly and use products specifically for this skin type, you will find your skin can improve. You may also find that a nutritionist's advice on your dietary habits could be more beneficial to your skin than just changing your beauty regime.

Sensitive

Your skin needs gentle products with natural ingredients. Your skin type may be any combination of the above, but needs extra TLC. But extra TLC may mean that less is more in the way of your beauty routine. A simple cleansing and moisturising product may be enough for you with no extra facials, exfoliation or even foundation. You could also find that you are more sensitive to some brands more than others.

Some of the best moisturisers are:

• Philosophy Hope in a Jar (for all skins): the name of this product was taken from a Mae West quote. Celebrity fan: Oprah Winfrey.

• Crème de la Mer (for dry skins). Celebrity fans: Sharon Stone, Jennifer Lopez.

• Dermalogica Active Moist (for oily skins)

All natural moisturisers for mature skins

• *Dr Hauschka Rose Day Cream (for mature skins): this soothing and balancing natural moisturiser is excellent for mature skins and smells wonderful. Celebrity fan: Madonna.*

• *Organic Pharmacy Rose Plus Anti-ageing Cream*

• *Aromatherapy Associates Renew Triple Rose Moisturiser: this blend of three varieties of rose essential oils is perfect for dry, dehydrated or older skins.*

Anti-ageing 'super' creams

These creams have all had intensive scientific research behind their development to create a new breed of super wrinkle-busting creams and anti-ageing high performance skin products. They combine cutting edge bio-technology, pharmaceutical grade ingredients and clinically proven technology.

• *Lancôme Primodiale Optimum Thermo-control SPF 15: this moisturiser is brilliant for more mature skins. Celebrity fan: Esther McVey.*

• *Elemis Pro-Collagen Marine Cream (Best Innovative Skincare Product 2006 CEW beauty Oscars): this cream helps smooth and reduce the appearance of fine lines and wrinkles.*

• *Dr Brandt Lineless Cream: this luxurious cream soothes and* hydrates, repairs and adds radiance to tired skins. It has concentrated levels of antioxidants to slow down the ageing process.

• *Elizabeth Arden Ceramide Plump Perfect Moisture Cream SPF 15: a non-surgical cosmetic alternative to help skin look youthful and healthy by plumping it up, helping reduce the appearance of fine lines and wrinkles.*

• *Yves Saint Laurent Lisse Expert Advanced Eye and Lip Intensive Anti-wrinkle Care: this helps smooth, plump and moisturise wrinkles. You can be accurate in targeting the specific area that needs help and you can use it twice daily under your make-up and before you use Yves Saint Laurent Touche Eclat concealer.*

• *Estee Lauder perfectionist (CP+) with Poly-collagen Peptides Correcting Serum for lines, wrinkles and age spots: you will see a line and wrinkle reduction from day one that will improve even more with regular use over the space of a month.*

• *Freeze 24.7 Ice cream Double Scoop Intensive Anti-ageing Moisturiser with protein extracts: it contains a gentle muscle contraction inhibitor to smooth fine lines and wrinkles. You use it morning and night.*

• *Natralox: all natural Botox style cream.*

• *Dr Denese Line-Erase*

• *StriVectin-SD Intensive Concentrate for the Face: originally sold as a stretch mark cream, women later found that this brand also had the ability to reduce the appearance of fine lines, wrinkles and crow's feet. For best results it must be used twice a day for at least a month. Celebrity fans: Jennifer Lopez, Jessica Simpson and Charlize Theron, Anthea Thurner, Val Garland (make-up artist to Sienna Miller and Drew Barrymore).*

• *Medik8 is a range of products with the latest dermaceutical peptide ingredients that have been researched and developed to act in the closest fashion possible to professional non-cosmetic procedures without the use of a needle. These include a painless gentler alternative to Botox (Pretox 3-HTP), a line filler (Prefill HA), a moisturiser, (Step 2 daily care 8-in-1 pre-SPF hydrator) and lip-plumping and eye-lifting treatments. All these treatments can be used underneath your regular skincare regime, twice a day, for at least a month to receive maximum benefits and thereafter once a month to maintain results. Celebrity fans: Donna Air, Halle Berry, Patsy Palmer and celebrity make-up artist John Gustafson.*

High street alternatives

If you can't afford the super-priced 'super' creams, there are high street alternatives that aim to deliver similar results.

• *Nivea Visage DNAge Cell Renewal Anti-age System Day/Night/Eye Cream: contains Folic Acid and Creatine, which encourage cell regeneration and also prevent further damage to the skin cells' DNA. This anti-aging system is perfect for women in the 40–55 age bracket as it helps skin with lost elasticity and firmness.*

• *Nivea Visage Age Reversal Intense Rejuvenating Care: this cream has vitamins C and E for skin cell renewal.*

• *Avon Anew Clinical ThermaFirm Facelifting Cream: this moisturising cream has been inspired by Thermage (see non-surgical procedures section). It lifts, tightens and tones. Results can be seen after three days.*

• *Skin Wisdom Instant Benefits Wrinkle Filler by Bharti Vyas at Tesco: this helps reduce the appearance of fine lines with light-reflecting particles and skin-smoothing ingredients.*

• *Skin Wisdom Instant Benefits Wrinkle Relax Concentrate by Bharti Vyas at Tesco: this is a 'click' pen that releases a concentrated serum to help tighten and plump skin and smooth fine lines.*

• *Avon Anew Clinical Laser: this has a unique pen-like roller ball applicator that helps reduce the appearance of spider veins, dark spots, under eye shadows. You can apply it every evening.*

• *Marks and Spencer Revival Cosmotox Serum Plus: this is a collagen-boosting skin-rejuvenating serum to help diminish facial wrinkles.*

• *Superdrug Optimum Wrinkle Reduction Serum Advance*

• *Olay Regenerist Daily Regenerating Serum: an anti-ageing regeneration and hydration amino-peptide complex. This can help your skin look younger in just three weeks.*

face cream helps with collagen production, relaxes lines and wrinkles and stimulates cell turnover. It also creates a perfect make-up base. Celebrity fans: Darcey Bussell, Bianca Jagger.

• *Guerlain Orchidee Imperiale Exceptional Complete Care Cream: this creates a radiance and softness. It smells sensual and feels deeply luxurious, with the Orchid as the symbol of eternal youth. The cream can help your skin to remain lastingly fresh and radiant just as the wild orchid does. Celebrity fans: Cate Blanchett, Yasmin le Bon.*

• *Crème De La Mer Moisturising Cream: this cream was conceived by Dr Max Huber – an aerospace*

Being 70 is no different from being 69. It's a round number, and there's something about roundness that has always appealed to me.

Elizabeth Taylor

One stop anti-ageing

These three 'miracle' creams are the Rolls Royce of face creams. This is reflected in the price but if you like luxury and can afford to pamper yourself, then go for it! They really do make your skin look and feel wonderful.

• *La Prairie Anti-aging Complex Cellular Intervention Cream: this*

physicist who suffered a horrific accident covering him with severe burns. He found nothing that could help his skin so he decided to help himself. Twelve years and many 1000s of experiments later, he perfected the cream that would give his skin a dramatically smoother, softer and more supple appearance. You apply it daily, day and night. This cream now has celebrity fans worldwide.

Moisturising serum

A moisturising serum is an extra boost for your skin you can use in addition to and on top of your moisturiser. You would use it before applying your make-up.

• *Nuxe Nuxuriance Brightening Intense Re-densifying Serum: great for mature skins.*

• *Dermalogica Skin Hydrating Booster: great for dry skins.*

• *Guerlain Super Aqua-serum Optimum Hydration Revitalizer*

• *Olay Regenerist Regenerating Serum and Lotion: these have the same formulas found in many of the top brands.*

• *Origins a Perfect World Antioxidant Moisturiser with White Tea: helps to prevent ageing. You use it twice a day.*

• *Caudalie Lifting Serum: an anti-ageing lifting and firming serum. Celebrity fans: Helen Mirren, Kirsten Dunst.*

Instant facelift products

As well as a serum, there are instant facelift products. These are for use when you look and feel tired. They are great to use before a party. A mask can also work wonders to give you an instant glow and lift.

• *Clarins Beauty Flash Balm: this is an instant pick-me-up to help minimize signs of tiredness and stress and make the skin look brighter and fresher. It also firms the skin and reduces the appearance of fine lines.*

• *Dr NV Perricone Face Firming Activator: with alpha lipoic acid and the magic ingredient DMAE, Dr Perricone's own formula. This product firms, tones and helps lift the skin. This is a daily use product for the improvement of muscle skin tone and will give you an instant boost. Celebrity fans: Hermione Norris, Miranda Richardson, Paula Abdul.*

• *Skindulgence 30 Minute Non-surgical Facelift: this literally gives you an instant lift.*

• *SK-11 Facial Treatment Mask. Celebrity fan: Madonna.*

Skin recovery whilst you sleep

Some products are specifically to help your skin recover whilst you sleep. What more could you want?

• *Guerlain Issima Midnight Secret late night recovery treatment: you apply this wonderful smelling cream to your cleansed face before going to sleep after a late/heavy night and however tired or hung over you may feel the following day you will still look glowing.*

• *Aromatherapy Associates Renew Rose and Sandalwood Facial Oil: a few drops of this natural oil can be used as a normal daily skincare routine or as an intensive treatment before going to bed. The mix of rose, sandalwood and primrose oils will make you not only smell good but be working whilst you sleep. This was the winner of 2006 Instyle best beauty buy.*

Eye cream

Can I use my moisturiser on my eyes as well as my face?

Some moisturisers are too rich to use around the delicate eye area as they may make your eyes puffy. This is why many brands have an eye product to team with the face cream. But the packaging will always have directions for use.

• *Superdrug Vitamin E Eye Contour Gel*

• *Skin Wisdom Age Reverse by Bharti Vyas for Tesco: an anti-wrinkle eye cream.*

• *StriVectin-SD eye cream: this is one of the new breed of super creams. Use twice daily and leave to be absorbed.*

Pre-party pick-me-ups for tired eyes

• *DR Harris and Co. Ltd. Crystal Eye Gel: this helps to reduce puffiness around the eyes.*

• *Clarins Eye Revive Beauty Flash: an instant pre-party lift.*

• *SK-11 signs eye mask: this skincare range is loved by celebrities including Madonna and really makes a difference. This is a great pre-party pick-me-up.*

• *Tea bags: these can be used, cooled and wet, to soothe puffy eyes. Any sort will work but you could try green tea and camomile as green tea contains antioxidants and camomile tea has soothing and healing properties.*

• *Cucumber: slices of cucumber have soothing properties when laid on tired or puffy eyes.*

Instant eye wrinkle reduction

• *Estee Lauder Perfectionist Power Correcting Patch for Deeper Eye Lines/Wrinkles: you can use these patches on all skin types. In just 20 minutes after placing the patch over the wrinkly area, you will see a definite reduction of the wrinkles and also a lifted effect.*

• *Avon Anew Clinical Eye Lift: a two part eye lift treatment that gives you an instant lift, reducing dark circles and crêpe-like skin.*

• *Medik8 Prelift X4: an injection free alternative to fade under-eye dark circles, smooth fine lines, lift bags and promote a bright, even skin tone.*

• *Hylexin: this is formulated for US beauty experts Bremenn Research labs, specifically to reduce the appearance of serious dark circles and under-eye puffiness. You apply this cream twice a day. Celebrity fan: Katherine Heigi.*

Post-party repair for tired eyes

• *Estee Lauder Advanced Night Repair Eye Recovery Complex: you can chill this in the fridge for 15 minutes before use to make it even more soothing.*

Spot and blemish removers

• *Origins Spot Remover Anti-blemish Treatment Gel: this works brilliantly and invisibly and won't aggravate more sensitive skins. Celebrity fan: Erin O' Connor.*

• *Dermalogica Medicated Clearing Gel. Celebrity fan: Kirsty Gallagher.*

• *Eve Lom Dynaspot Lotion: this spot treatment really works. Celebrity fans: Elizabeth Jagger, Dannii Minogue, Stella Tennant, Helena Christianson.*

• *Clinique Anti-blemish Solutions Clear Blemish Gel*

• *Medik8 Red Alert: a professional strength anti-redness formula to help fade and clear thread veins, skin redness, rosacea and bruises.*

Multi purpose skin relief 'healers'

These can be used on dry skin patches anywhere, and soothe irritated skin. You can use 'skin healer' creams as often as you wish, especially if you have mild skin problems and would prefer to avoid using a cortisone or steroid cream to suppress the itch.

• *Cashmere Beauty Rapid Recovery Cream: this fast acting relief cream with anti-inflammatory, antioxidant and moisturising properties can be used for anti-ageing, scar tissue, skin redness and irritation, psoriasis and excema.*

• *Eucerin dry skin range: this range of products help prevent, care for and treat dry skin and dry skin conditions such as excema.*

• *Rio Rosa Mosqueta Oil: this natural oil really does help problem skin. You can use it daily or just at night.*

• *Elizabeth Arden Eight Hour Cream: this is one of the most popular products in the Elizabeth Arden range and the celebrities' choice of product to take to a desert island as it moisturises, can soothe burns and even be used as a lip gloss too.*

• *Liz Earle Superbalm Concentrate. Celebrity fans: Laura Bailey. Tara Palmer-Tomkinson and Sharon Osbourne.*

• *Organic Apoteke Droseros Face and Body Spritz: a rose scented moisturising mist with homeopathic ingredients for soothing dry, irritated or sun-damaged skin.*

Other healing remedies

• *Arnica 30*

• *SinEcch Arnica Tablets (Especially for post-op healing.)*

• *DCL Europe Post-Peel Quick Recovery Healing Ointment*

• *Lavender essential oil*

• *Tisserand Aromatherapy Lavender Gel*

Lip care

What can I use to reduce the severity of cold sore outbreaks naturally?

• *Liquorice balm: application of this balm helps reduce the severity of cold sores.*

• *Virulite CS Innovative Cold Sore Treatment: this is a pocket sized laser that you direct at cold sore outbreaks. It definitely helps. I use this in conjunction with the liquorice balm.*

I get dry lips.
For dry or chapped lips try lip balms:

• *Burt's Bees Beeswax Lip Balm*

• *Rose and Co Lipsalve*

UV protection

I know that I must wear a daily sunscreen, so can I buy a combined sunscreen and moisturiser?

Sunburn causes instant skin ageing, so you should wear a daily sunscreen product of at least factor 15. You can choose a moisturiser with a built in sunscreen.

• *L'Occitane Shea Butter Ultra Moisturising Care SPF 15*

• *Neutrogena Visibly Refined Pore Refining Moisturiser SPF 15*

• *Neutrogena Visibly Young Day Cream SPF 15*

• *Clinique Super City Block SPF 25 Oil-free Daily Face Protector*

Or you can wear a dedicated sunscreen. One that you would put on to sunbathe.

• *Nivea Sun Moisturising Facial Sunscreen SPF 30*

• *Lancaster Precious Sun SPF 15: although expensive, I think this is one of the best facial suntan lotions on the market as it not only protects your skin but helps care for it with its cocktail of clever ingredients to support the skin repair/renew system. I have been using this on my face on all of my visits to tropical holiday destinations and loved it.*

Anti-ageing alternatives

So you now have a regular skincare routine and can see an improvement in your skin. What else can you do to combat ageing?

You can eat healthily.

You need to eat fruit, vegetables and foods rich in:
• Amino acids. Found in meat.
• Beta carotene (the pigment that converts to vitamin A to help create new cells), found in sweet potatoes, carrots, apricots, peaches and nectarines.

• Bycopene (helps prevent premature ageing), found in tomatoes, pink grapefruit and watermelon.
• Omega 3 fatty acids (helps moisturisation of the skin), found in oily fish, walnuts and flaxeed oil.
• Vitamin C (helps build new collagen). In current medical studies, it has been shown that taking 3 gm of vitamin C daily as an antioxidant can help combat ageing. Found in citrus fruits and berries.
• Selenium. Found in fish, red meat, chicken, grains and eggs.
• Vitamin E (antioxidant that combats cell damage and free radicals). Found in nuts, seeds and avocados and green vegetables.
• Zinc. Medical studies have shown that taking zinc can affect the skin cell structure in a positive way for anti-ageing. Zinc is found mostly in meat, fish, and other animal products. It's especially high in oysters, crabmeat, red meat, chicken, and eggs. You could take a daily zinc tablet, but never on an empty stomach as zinc can cause an upset stomach. Doses should be small.
• Folic acid. Medical studies have shown that taking 400 mcg daily can also help the regeneration of the skin cells. Found in foods that contain folate, the natural form of the acid, including fortified breakfast cereals, dried beans, leafy green vegetables and orange juice.

It is important to consult your doctor before taking any vitamins or supplements.

Anti-ageing supplements

You can take extra supplements that are specifically for anti-ageing.

• *Imedeen Systemic Skin Solution Time Perfection: this course of tablets helps to improve skin tone and combats ageing, especially formulated for mature and sun-damaged skin. You take two tablets daily. Celebrity fans: Joanna Lumley, Laura Bailey, Naomi Campbell.*

• *Vitalize Pro-ferm+ Internal Care: a food supplement that is taken in conjunction with the use of the pro-ferm range. The Deep Revitalizing Treatment and the Instant Lifting Serum, both with hyaferm and glucaferm, are my favourites in the range. This combination of the cosmeceutical creams and pills containing vitamins, minerals and antioxidants can make a difference to the elasticity, firmness and hydration of your skin.*

What else should I do on a regular basis?

• Keep suntanning on the face minimal.
• Keep cleansing, toning and moisturising regularly.
• Drink 2 litres of water a day.
• Drink less alcohol.
• Don't smoke.

• Sleep on your back. If you sleep on your side or face down, the pressure on your face causes the skin to wrinkle, especially the nasal-labial fold that is the line down from the nose to the mouth. Laughter lines or crow's feet can also form from sleeping this way. So if you wake up and find yourself on your side or front, turn over again onto your back. (Yes it sounds daft, but I know of celebrities who actually do this!)

Facials

Facials cleanse, tone and moisturise the face. They help the circulation and in bringing fresh blood supplies to the skin, they can make you look fresher and reduce the appearance of fine lines and wrinkles by temporarily tightening and toning the skin. Salon and spa facials are likely to be more effective than over-the-counter ones for use at home but all will give you a temporary 'feel good' factor.

Mini-peels

A mini-peel is more intense than a facial and will help renew your skin cells by exfoliating the surface layer.

• *Olay Regenerist Thermal Skin Polisher: this self-heats and exfoliates. You can use this every day to give your face a cleansing mini-peel.*

85

• *MD skincare by Dr Dennis Gross Alpha Beta Daily Face Peel. Celebrity fan: Jessica Alba.*

• *Estee Lauder Perfectionist Peel Two Step Enzyme Activating Treatment: this at home peel will give the same result as a professional 30 per cent glycolic acid peel in only one treatment.*

• *Avon Anew Clinical Two Step Facial Peel: you can use this two-step treatment with glycolic acid, fruit extracts and honey every other day to re-texturise and smooth skin.*

• *Eve Lom Cleanser with glycolic acid : this will gently remove dead skin cells too.*

Micro-dermabrasion

You could try at-home micro-dermabrasion that will also help to renew and resurface the skin.

• *Dr Brandt Skincare Micro-dermabrasion In a Jar: this can be used up to twice a week to smooth fine lines, help control acne and improve mild scarring. It can also be used on the arms, hands and décolleté.*

• *L'Oreal ReFinish Micro-Dermabrasion Kit*

• *Boots Time Delay Two Step Micro-dermabrasion Kit: part of Boots' award-winning anti-aging range. This new formulation will help reduce the appearance of large pores*

and visibly reduce the appearance of fine lines within just two weeks, leaving skin soft and radiant.

What about facial exercises?

Regular facial exercises may prevent or help wrinkles as the facial support muscles support the skin but could also cause new facial lines to develop whilst doing the exercises.

Cosmetic acupuncture

If you're looking for an all natural lifting treatment that really does make a difference then you can try cosmetic acupuncture. You will need to have a course of at least six once a month to really make a difference. But as with any course of treatments you will need to maintain it. It's worth finding a well-established therapist with a good reputation for acupuncture procedures, such as my personal favourite, Stephen Langley at the Hale Clinic in London.

Is there anything else new?

In the USA, the search for the holy grail of everlasting youthful looks has turned to a high tech company called Dermagenetics. This company tests your DNA and formulates a face cream specifically suited to your unique skin cell DNA. They test your cells for collagen breakdown, photo-ageing, wrinkling, skin ageing and overall health. This test and cream costs around the same as a top of the market luxury brand but it could be quite 'cool' to say that your face cream was matched specially to your DNA, although it has yet to be proved whether this new system actually works.

An at-home anti-ageing mini 'spa' machine

• *Galvanic Spa II: this machine can tone you from top to toe, helping you look younger with healthier hair and a more toned body. The galvanic current helps the body absorb the accompanying products dependant on which part of the body you are treating.*

Prescription creams

• *Retin-A: this is the only proven effective anti-ageing cream on the market that can dramatically affect how the skin actually looks. It renews the skin cells by allowing new cells to grow after causing old outer layer of skin to be shed. You would use it nightly for a prescribed period of time and then maybe twice weekly, according to how you react to it. It can, though, cause your skin to become sensitive and you must always use a sun protection factor min 15+ afterwards.*

Non-surgical procedures

'It is sad to grow old but nice to ripen.'

Lauren Bacall

Although you can never look too thin or too young in Hollywood, there has been a gradual shift away from 'nip/tuck surgery' to having gentle tweaks without going under the knife. The new message is that it is now cool to be comfortable with your age, with the help of non-surgical procedures giving a subtler, softer look. The aim is to look naturally beautiful like Sharon Stone, Kristin Scott-Thomas or the ever glamorous and sexy Sophia Loren.

'I will never cut my face. I just do a lot of anti-ageing things to slow the process down.'

Eva Longoria

When I am consulted by my clients, I recommend and work with many of the worlds' top cosmetic surgeons, skin doctors and beauticians, so I see and hear about all the latest treatments. For the following pages I consulted with Bassim Matti FRCS (Fellow of Royal College of Surgeons) who is a consultant plastic surgeon and the UK secretary of the International Society of Aesthetic Plastic Surgery society (ISAPS), the British Association of Plastic Surgeons (BAPS) and the British Association of Aesthetic Plastic Surgeons (BAAPS).

The non-surgical procedures I have mentioned here are, in his opinion, the best currently on the market and can help combat ageing.

Non-surgical options work best as methods of preventing ageing rather than ways of removing the signs of ageing that already exist. Non-surgical techniques are procedures that do not require surgical incisions or cutting into the skin. The results are mostly immediate. Anaesthetic and recovery from the surgery is not required, although some do need skin healing recovery time.

These treatments will *improve* the current you, maybe ironing out a wrinkle or two, filling in a line or smoothing your skin.

As with most beauty treatments they do need maintenance top-ups to be repeated a couple of times a year.

So what are the non-surgical options?

Skin peels

A skin peel renews skin cells by peeling away the very top layer of the skin surface. A peel can improve skin imperfections from acne scarring to fine lines and sun damage.

Are there different sorts of peels?

A mild skin peel contains alpha hydroxy glycolic acid. After a light or mild skin peel you will not need any healing time. Alpha hydroxyl acid (AHA) peels are good at reducing the appearance of fine lines and wrinkles and improving the tone, colour and texture of the skin. You could have a light peel done as often as once a month up to six months and then maintenance peels every two to three months afterwards.

A medium peel is applied in the same way as the mild skin peel. But it can sting briefly when applied. It is good for fine lines and wrinkles and will have a longer lasting impact than the mild peel.

A deep acid peel contains 20–30 per cent glycolic acid and you will need to be out of action for at least ten days for recovery time as your face will look like it has been burnt. It can improve sun damaged skin, fine lines and wrinkles and mild acne scars.

A laser peel or skin resurface is a strong and invasive peel and it takes about a week to heal. It can help age lines, sun damage, skin texture and give your skin a more toned and taut appearance.

Can there be any negative side effects?

You should never use a formula with more than ten per cent glycolic acid at home as you could end up with facial burns.

A chemical peel gives a smoother, brighter complexion but should not be used too often. The continuous action of artificially creating cell renewal will stop the skin's natural ability to heal itself and produce healthy collagen and elastin.

Scarring is more likely to develop with a medium or deep laser peel or laser resurfacing than any of the mild peels.

A peel can trigger off cold sores if you are prone to them.

You will be more sensitive to the sun. You should try to avoid the sun for at least six months after a major peel.

Peels and laser resurfacing can cause pigmentation problems and may be more successful on fair skinned people than dark.

Laser treatments

These are used for hair removal, tattoo removal and the treatment of scarring, acne scarring, fine lines, wrinkles and thread veins.

Are there different sorts of laser?

• *Fraxel is a new laser treatment that works very well on pigmentation changes, fine lines, wrinkles and acne scars. After* *multiple treatments the skin can be seen to improve and also tighten. It can last up to 18 months after at least three treatments*

Does it hurt?

Yes, and it needs a topical anaesthetic cream to be applied to help numb the skin. As with most laser treatments you will feel a burning sensation, although some surgeries/salons use a cooling device simultaneously to the laser treatment.

How long will it take to heal?

Around three to five days. You can't wear make-up and swelling, redness, dryness and flaking are all possible.

What can go wrong?

Skin discolouration and scarring if not used correctly.

• *IPL (intense pulsed light): this laser treatment works for fine lines, brown spots and changes of pigmentation, birth marks and scars, tattoo removal, broken capillaries, hair removal and skin rejuvenation.*

This laser treatment is gentler and has no recovery time, although you might get some redness immediately afterwards. You need a series of treatments over weeks. You can see an improvement usually after four to six treatments.

These lasers both deliver an intense light to a specific area.

• *Aculight: a laser light therapy to treat thread veins and rosacea.*

• *Nlite V laser treatment*

• *YAG: this laser creates a beam of high intensity light that penetrates deeply into the skin tissue causing a 'zone' of heat. This 'trauma' stimulates collagen/fibroblasts and results in tighter, more youthful looking skin. This treatment can be uncomfortable but the laser's heat is minimised by a cooling device used at the same time. Around six treatments given once a month are usually needed. After any laser treatment sun exposure is always best avoided.*

New facelift alternatives

• *Thermage and Polaris: these treatments use radio waves to penetrate the skin and heat the collagen under the skin causing the skin to shrink and tighten. This can help give the skin a fresher look after multiple sessions and then maintenance treatments. This can work well on the neck. It can last up to 18 months.*

• *Isolagen: in this cell replacement treatment your own cells are taken from behind the ear and then grown in the lab. They are then injected back into your skin to create and rebuild new collagen wherever necessary. The treatment should give smoother skin, improved texture, tone and elasticity. Success though, is not guaranteed nor permanent. Results can appear three months after treatment, and last up to 12–18 months. There should be a steady improvement in skin texture and tone.*

Injected absorbable non-permanent fillers

Collagen is the best known proven non permanent filler that has stood the test of time with rare allergic reactions. It is used most often for the lips. Your body naturally contains collagen. As you age, the collagen in your skin starts to diminish and fine lines and wrinkles start to form. Injections of collagen work instantly and can last from three to six months.

What are some of the absorbable non-permanent fillers?

• *Restylane: this is based on hyaluronic acid and is a non-animal bio-engineered hyaluronic gel that is the most widely used filler. There are different versions of Restylane for separate areas, such as fine lines and deeper wrinkles on the face, the neck and lips.*

Hylaform, Hyalan and Hydrafill fill out medium and fine lines; Puragen and Puragen Plus are other options.

All of these are trademarked brand names of absorbable non-permanent fillers. They all contain hyaluronic acid. This is a natural substance already present in the body's connective tissues, which helps keep the moisture locked in. It diminishes as you get older.

Laresse: this is the latest non-animal derivative filler that doesn't contain hyaluronic acid. It can last up to six months. This is best for lips.

Are there questions I should ask?
• What is the filler you are going to use on me derived from? Animal, natural or synthetic?
• What are the side effects?
• Could I have a reaction to it?
• Could I be allergic to it?
• What can be done if I am?
• Can it be removed?
• Will I get bruising or swelling after these filler treatments?

You may get minimal swelling, and there is the possibility of bruising as there is with any injection.

Injected semi-permanent fillers

Radiesse: this is usually used for nose to mouth lines.

Nu Fill: this provokes the skin to generate collagen.

Sculptra: this is injected to stimulate new collagen to fill out hollows and deep wrinkles and the results are gradual over months. You need a series of three treatments.

These are all semi-permanent and are generally safe but can cause problems such as lumps. They aren't good for the lips but are better for filling out cheeks and hollows.

Should I choose permanent, semi-permanent or absorbable non-permanent?
Bassim Matti suggests always choosing absorbable non-permanent fillers as they are absorbed gradually by the body and are safer. Semi-permanent and permanent fillers can cause a reaction and are very difficult to remove.

What are the possible side effects?
The side effects of semi-permanent or permanent fillers can be scarring or lumps and bumps. You may need surgery to remove the filler, leaving scarring.

Botox

Botox is the most commonly used non-surgical procedure of all and it really does iron out crow's feet, wrinkles, forehead lines and frown lines between the eyebrows. But it looks so much better when used with restraint, as it can leave so many women's faces devoid of any expression. As with most things in life, less is always more.

Botox is a muscle relaxing substance that is injected into the facial muscles. It creates temporary paralysis, causing the muscles under the skin to relax so that forehead lines, crow's feet, frown lines, smoker's lip fine lines, downward droopy mouth corners and neck lines look ironed out.

Even under arm sweating can disappear (some Hollywood stars have this done before the Oscars). Botox lasts around three to four months and can take years off your face virtually overnight. It takes a couple of days to kick in.

Fat dissolve techniques

• Lipostabile: dissolves fat in the area it is injected into. But this is not yet licensed in the UK as there could be long term side effects that no one yet knows about.

• SmartLipo laser: this is less extreme than liposuction and offered as a 'lunch hour' fat removal

treatment. A laser probe inserted into the skin heats up and melts the membranes of the fat cells, causing the now liquid fat to be excreted through the natural metabolic process over 12 to 16 weeks. This treatment has passed safety tests and is available in a few countries so far including the UK, but does not yet have approval from the FDA (American Food and Drug Administration) although this is not a legal requirement in the UK for it to be administered.

What questions should I ask my surgeon or practitioner?

• What are your qualifications and training?
• What professional bodies do you belong to?
• How long have you been practising and where?
• What do you recommend for me and why?
• What results can I expect?
• What are the risks?
• What are the negative aspects to this treatment?
• What is the healing and recovery time?
• Is there anything I should avoid doing afterwards?

Teeth

You can instantly improve your facial appearance with a great smile and good teeth.

 Do you look after your teeth as well as you do your hair?

Do you...

• Have regular dentist check-ups and teeth cleans?
• Clean your teeth twice a day?
• Change your toothbrush regularly?
• Floss daily?
• Avoid smoking?
• Brush your tongue?
• Drink lots of water?

If keeping your teeth healthy and clean is not enough for you, you can also improve their appearance. But even though many of the Hollywood stars have whiter, more even looking teeth than those they started out with, perfection isn't really necessary. Lauren Hutten went through her career as a top model with a gap between her front teeth and Madonna also has a gap. It is always much more interesting to look slightly imperfect. If you would like to improve your teeth, however, even just a little bit, there are many instant options.

I don't like the shape of my teeth.

The dentist can file with a sort of mini electric sander any chipped or uneven teeth or change the size of your teeth with bonding. Bonding is a plastic that can be used to change instantly chipped teeth, enlargen teeth and fill in small gaps. It will last for quite a few years but can chip and discolour with time.

My teeth are crooked.

You can even out your crooked teeth, reshaping them with bonding or veneers. Veneers are porcelain facades that are created to fit permanently around the front of your own teeth to create a more uniform shape and colour. A tiny bit off the edges of the tooth will need to be filed down to give room for the porcelain veneer. The veneers will give you a brighter, whiter and better smile and can be done within seven to fourteen days.

I didn't wear braces when I was a child – is it too late now?

It's never too late! I had my teeth straightened as my thirty-something birthday present to myself, wearing braces for a year. In fact I wore clear fixed braces and no one noticed them, even when I was appearing on TV. Eating anything crispy like an apple or a carrot was tricky and kissing was also not too high on the agenda, but I am so much happier with my straight teeth now. Also it is much easier to floss and brush them to keep them clean and healthy when they are not so crowded.

❝The best colour in the whole world is the one that looks good on you.❞

Coco Chanel

How about teeth whitening?

Hydrogen peroxide solution is painted on the teeth and subjected to a laser that speeds up the bleaching process. This procedure can lighten the teeth by up to 11 shades. You can get the Hollywood smile like this but it can leave your teeth more sensitive. There are many methods of whitening and 'Zoom' can cause less sensitivity than other whitening methods.

You cannot choose the exact shade of your new tooth whiteness with a laser whitening treatment. It's not an exact science. So don't believe a dentist when he says you can. Also all teeth whitening will fade again with time.

Can toothpaste help?

There are now all sorts of whitening toothpastes on the market. Some claim to help protect against ageing with vitamin E or folic acid included in the ingredients. Others claim to whiten and can be used occasionally or on a regular basis according to how non-abrasive the ingredients are. My favourite for regular use is Janina Whitening toothpaste.

If you brush your teeth and floss regularly, not only will you have a great smile but also nice fresh breath. However good you look and feel, bad breath is a big turn off.

Choosing the right colour for your face

The moment you become more hormonal, at the time of becoming a young woman or reaching the menopause, you will find that your skin tone, eye colour and hair colour all change. As you age, your hair may become darker, duller or grey, your skin will be affected by the environment and sun damage and your eye colour may also change slightly. This is why you mustn't stick to the same make-up colours, hair colour tints or even the same clothes' colours over the years. The colours of the clothes that you wear affect how you look and feel. They can affect your mood, your energy and how others view you. Remember, you only have 30 seconds to create a first impression when you meet someone! So you don't want to look dull or boring or conversely too 'over the top'.

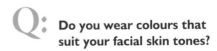

Q: **Do you wear colours that suit your facial skin tones?**

Everyone has skin tones that can be categorised simply as warm (yellow-toned) or cool (pink-toned). Yellow-toned skins tan easily, whilst pink-toned skins usually have difficulty tanning or are freckly. So when you consider your hair colour and your make-up and your clothes you need to think about your skin tone.

I look tired and drained some days.

Black can drain the colour from your face and make you feel and look tired and older.

If you have to wear black, team it with a colour near your face to compliment your skin tones. You can use jewellery, scarves, shawls, or a glimpse of a t shirt underneath a jacket.

I prefer not to be noticed so I wear beige.

Beige is a non-threatening safe colour but it is important to try various tones of beige near your face and see which ones drain your skin colour and which ones lift. A warmer beige will work better on a yellow-toned skin.

I am frightened of wearing colour.

Colour can help you feel and look more youthful. Even if you are scared to wear bright red there is no reason why you can't wear other flattering shades, such as pastels or even turquoise, that will improve your spirits, confidence and how you appear to others. But choose your colours with care; some may only need

to be worn as an 'accent' colour under a jacket or as an accessory as the colour could overpower you if too vibrant.

I like certain colours even if they don't suit me.

But which shade of the colour suits you? For example, you may say you *like* pink but it doesn't seem to suit you. Have you tried putting a pink with blue undertones such as baby pink or fuchsia near your skin, and then trying a pink with yellow undertones such as a coral? One will look much better and 'illuminate' your face. If you have a pink-toned skin the blue-toned pink will look best and if you have a yellow-toned skin then the coral will look best. The same goes for your foundation and lipstick tones.

I don't understand how to choose the right shade.

The correct colour should light up your face. It will make you look fresher and younger. It will bring out the colour of your eyes. It will make people notice *you*, not what you're wearing.

The following is a basic colour guide to help you choose the colours that suit you. You m ay find that a certain colour, even if you now know the correct shade or tone, may need to be paler or darker to be best for you. It's quite subtle and you will find that all colours are different in daylight than in artificial lighting. That's why you always need to check both your clothes and your make-up in daylight if the lighting in your bathroom or bedroom isn't very good.

Wearing the best colour for you is not an exact science and I would never advocate any woman walking around clothes shops with their suggested specific colour swatches. But I do think that from these basic suggestions you can understand why some colours will work better with *your* skin tones than other ones, and avoid making the mistake of buying clothes in colours that don't suit you. (Black is not a mistake, it's just a safe option).

Dark hair with tanned skin, or skin that tans easily

You are best in clear strong colours. Celebrity example: Jennifer Lopez, Halle Berry , Elizabeth Hurley.
purple
bright red
electric blue
emerald
bright turquoise
fuchsia
yellow
black
white

Brown or dark brown hair, red hair, fair hair with pale skin, freckles or skin that doesn't tan easily

Celebrity examples: Nicole Kidman, Julianne Moore, Erin O'Connor.
brown
green
gold
khaki
turquoise
charcoal
purple
white

Fair hair, with golden skin that tans easily

You look best in warm-toned colours with some depth and life in them, rather than cool-toned ones. For example, a warm shade of camel is better than a dull flat shade of camel as this will be draining.
Celebrity examples: Scarlett Johansson; Kate Winslet, Elle Macpherson.
mid-blue,
mid-green
yellow-red
turquoise
mid-brown
warm camel
light grey
taupe
coral
cream

Light 'Nordic' blonde hair, pale skin with pinky tones that doesn't tan easily
These look best in clear 'cool' pastels.
Celebrity examples: Grace Kelly, Gwyneth Paltrow.
baby pink
baby blue
lilac
pale turquoise
primrose
white
icy grey
eau de nil
maroon
pinky brown

'I love fashion. I love when people put me in it. And God knows, I'm slowly getting better at putting stuff together myself.'

Jennifer Aniston

Accessories for your face shape

 Do you know what earrings to wear to complement your face shape?

My face shape is oval.
Celebrity examples: Scarlett Johansson, Beyonce Knowles, Charlize Theron.
You can wear any style earrings unless you have a short neck, in which case keep away from long dangly ones.

My face shape is square, with my cheekbones in line with my jaw.
Celebrity examples: Sarah Jessica Parker, Paris Hilton.
You can wear earrings that do not echo your facial squareness. Softer shapes which hang are good or rounded shapes such as hoops.

My face shape is rectangular with a wide jaw.
Celebrity examples: Jennifer Aniston, Minnie Driver.
Do not wear earrings that attract attention to your jawline. You would be better with studs or small earrings.

My face shape is an inverted triangle with cheekbones and a small pointy chin.
Celebrity examples: Kate Moss, Cameron Diaz, Jennifer Lopez.
You can wear any big earrings from hoops to drops that attract attention to, or broaden your jawline.

My face shape is round.
Celebrity examples: Gwen Stefani, Christina Aguilera, Renee Zellweger, Kirsten Dunst.
Do not echo your face shape by wearing hoop or round shaped earrings. Keep to small, understated and subtle or long and dangly.

❝When anyone asked what I wanted to be when I grew up, I'd say 'Blond' because to me that represented beauty.❞

Jamie-Lynn Sigler

Hair

Hair and how you feel are often related. A bad hair day can make you feel unattractive whilst great hair makes you feel positive and good about yourself and therefore more attractive. How your hair is groomed can also influence how you are perceived. Sleek equals being in control and professional. Curly or wavy can indicate sensuality and sexiness and being more relaxed.

'Put up' hair can make you feel more glamorous and draws attention to the neck and décolleté. Hair colour too can give off signals. Do blondes have a better time? Are redheads only seen as 'gingers' or as sexy sultry temptresses? Apparently red shows individuality, strength and sensuality whilst brunettes are seen to be more serious and sophisticated.

What is the best hairstyle for my face shape?
Knowing your face shape will help you choose the best hairstyle, make-up and spectacles for you. See the section on determining your face shape on pages 48-49.

My face is round.
Choose hairstyles that are layered and cut into, taking away the weight of the hair, creating a style that lengthens and frames the face without making it appear rounder.

My face is long.
Your hairstyle should help shorten the face with a fringe or a cut such as a textured chin length bob.

My face is oval.

Yours is the perfect face shape that suits all hairstyles. However, your age, together with your size (fat or thin) and neck length (short or long) will affect your choice of style. If you are over 50 then it is probably better not to have one-length long hair as it will drag your features down and be more ageing.

My face is square.

Choose a hairstyle that softens the square angles of your features. A layered or soft cut that frames the face will be best for you. Do not have a heavy fringe or short bob.

My face is rectangular.

Choose a hairstyle that softens your features as with the square shaped face.

My face is triangular (narrower at top of head).

Choose a hairstyle that broadens the top of your head and slims your jaw.

My face is triangular (narrower at jaw).

You can wear most hairstyles just as the oval face.

My nose is protruding or too large/too long.

Balance your nose with a fringe or a hairstyle that has volume over the forehead. Do not have a centre parting as it will draw attention to your nose. Very flat hair at the back of your head will emphasise your nose when you are seen in profile.

I have a weak chin.

Make sure that your haircut does not stop at a point higher than your chin, drawing attention to it. A haircut which is soft and framing around the face and jawline is more flattering.

My ears stick out.

You need a haircut that gives width and volume around your ears. Never wear your hair tucked behind your ears or cut in a short style around your ears. It's all about illusion and tricking the eye.

I have a high forehead.

The best way to disguise a high forehead is with a fringe. It doesn't have to be a heavy fringe: it can be a wispy or layered fringe.

Q: Does your hairstyle flatter your body shape?

I'm fatter than I would like to be.
Do not wear your hair in any style that creates extra fullness around your face. Keep to sleek, flattering styles. Not too long, not too big, not too curly. Your hair colour can be broken up with lowlights or highlights around the face.

I'm thinner than I would like to be.
Your hairstyle can help create volume around your face. You could try chunky wedge styles, layered styles around the face, messy 'beach-style' or tousled, big hair.

Beach hair effect products

- *Bumble and Bumble Surf Spray: this spritz creates sexy beach hair even when you're not on holiday. Celebrity fans: Teri Hatcher, Erin O'Connor, Sienna Miller.*

- *Fudge Unleaded Rewire: a daily leave-in moisture spritz to create a beach hair look. Celebrity fan: Kelly Osbourne.*

I've just lost lots of weight.
Long hair can make you look even thinner and drag down your facial features, so a bob or a layered cut would be more flattering.

I have a short neck.
If you have too much hair around your shoulders your neck will look shorter still.

 How can you look ten years younger with a new hairstyle?

I haven't changed my hairstyle for years.
As you age, you change. We all do. Your weight may remain the same but you will be carrying it in different places, and your face shape will be the same but certain features may become more prominent. And of course there is gravity which is always helping everything go south. So your hairstyle needs to lift your features, and complement your face shape. What suited you 20 years ago is very unlikely to do the same for you now.

'My hair had grown completely out of shape and when I looked in the mirror, I felt so depressed. So I started looking at middle-aged women who did have very short hair. That's when I realised I'd go for it.'

Francesca Annis

A hairstyle change is always exciting. It can totally change you. Victoria Beckham and Madonna both caused a stir when they unmasked their new bobs, even though Madonna's was later revealed to be a wig.

My hair is still the same length as it has been for the last 20 years.
Long hair drags your face down and can be ageing. Hair framing your face or a chin length bob will take off ten years.

I would like to wear my long hair up for a party but it has lots of flyaway short ends.
You can use hairspray to keep it in place. Either by spraying straight onto your styled hair or onto your hand and then smoothing over your hair.

Many celebrity hairdressers' choice of spray is Elnett hairspray. It holds but can still be brushed out at the end of the night.

My hair has been the same colour for the last 20 years.
Never try to go back to your original hair colour as you age. You may find that a warmer or softer shade is more flattering, especially in the case of red heads.

cutting ties with your old life. Your choice of hairstyle can define how people will see you. Do you want to be seen as sexy, business-like, or feminine?

Anna Wintour, editor of US *Vogue*, wears her hair in a bob that says

> *I'm not offended by all the dumb blonde jokes, because I know I'm not dumb – and I also know that I'm not blonde.*
>
> **Dolly Parton**

My hair is grey.
Never ever have your hair dyed one flat colour to get rid of the grey. The more extreme the colour the more you will look washed out and actually older, not younger. Keep your hair colour close to your original colour. If it was dark, don't let it be densely one colour, but add some lowlights. If it was red or blonde you could add some highlights. This streakiness will also help to make the constant problem of visible regrowth less apparent.

So what are you going to do first to create that new you? A new haircut, or a new body shape?

Many women, when suddenly faced with life on their own after a partnership break-up, cut their hair off, or have a radical re-style. Cutting off your locks is as much to do with being perceived as a 'new you' as

'sexy, well groomed, controlled and business-like'. Even *very* short hair can look sexy and feminine, when on the right shaped face with good cheekbones. Sharon Stone and Sienna Miller are celebrities who looked great with very short hair.

Your hair colour too can change how you feel about yourself and how others see you.

'I feel more chic when I have really dark hair.'

Lindsay Lohan

Q: Do you care for your hair properly?

'Don't over blow-dry your hair, use nylon combs or brushes or over wash it. The natural oils are good for it.'
Jerry Hall

I would like to use only natural products on my hair.

• *Amazonia Preciosa by Surya: a Brazilian range of shampoos, conditioners and treatments that not only smell exotic but that will also help to give you healthy, glossy hair naturally.*

• *MOP Glisten Shampoo: moisturises and helps to give extra shine naturally. Celebrity fans: Lucy Liu, Drew Barrymore, Helena Christiansen.*

My hair colour fades so quickly after my visit to the hairdressers. Are there products that would help maintain it better?

Shampoo, conditioners and protection for coloured hair:

• *Aussie Colour Mate shampoo and conditioner*

• *Redken Color Extend Conditioner. Celebrity fan: Kim Cattrall.*

• *John Frieda Brilliant Brunette, Sheer Blonde and Radiant Red shampoos*

I swim every day.
Cover your hair with a protecting product and wear a swim hat.

• *Kerastase Crème Aqua Resist: for coloured hair swim protection.*

I have lots of hair but it's very fine and flyaway. It needs some more body put into it.
I use these products to give volume and body for my own fine hair.

• *Phytovolume Actif Maximising Volume Spray: for fine and limp hair.*

• *Kerastase Volumactive Spray*

I don't know how to blow-dry my hair to create volume.
• Towel dry your hair first.
• Then add some product for volume or extra hold.
• Don't hold the hairdryer on full heat too close to your hair or for too long, as it dries it out.
• Turn your head up upside down and brush it whilst drying. It gives volume.
• You can scrunch your hair as you dry it, if you would like messy wavy bed style hair.

For scrunch drying with volume and hold:

• *Joico Joigel Styling Gel Medium Hold: for all hair types. A styling* product for volume and body and to redefine curls. It's quick drying and doesn't flake. Celebrity fan: Sarah Jessica Parker.

I can't blow-dry my hair so that it's sleek.

To get best results, it's important to point the nozzle of the hairdryer down the direction of the hair shaft, smoothing it with the directional hot air flow and with the brush. Aim the hairdryer nozzle very close onto the hair wrapped over the brush. Finish off with cold air. It helps shine and also set.

I blow-dry my hair every day.

If you have to blow-dry your hair each day then I suggest you use the dryer on a low heat setting.

A powerful hairdryer will help your hairstyle and cut look its best. The higher the wattage, the stronger the airflow, enabling your hair to be dried quicker with less heat. Most professional hairdryers aren't less than 1800 watts.

It is always best to use a lower heat setting and if your hairdryer has a nozzle you can direct the heat exactly to where you want it – where you have the hair over the brush.

TIPS

Favourite hairdryer

Remington hairdryers. They are powerful and come in all shapes and sizes from daily use ones to travel size.

Hairbrushes

The Rolls Royce of hairbrushes are Mason Pearson made of natural bristle. But you can also get natural bristle ones on the high street.

Favourite straightening irons

Ghd Professional Ceramic Straighteners

I use hair straighteners most days.

You must protect your hair from the heat with a product.

For use with hair straighteners: these products protect and help style and smooth.

• TRESemme Heat Defence Styling spray

• TRESemme Smoothing Serum

• L'Oreal Hot Style Constructor

The most efficient straightening irons should be hot enough that they do not require you to run them over your hair more than once, so that you don't overheat and damage the hair.

My hair is curly and difficult to manage.

• Bumble and Bumble Curl Conscious Curl Crème for Medium to Thick hair: it helps curls and reduces frizz.

For afro or mixed race hair
• Twisted Sista Curl Activator: helps smooth, moisturise and create curls without frizz.

My hair has frizz and is difficult to manage.

There are many anti-frizz products to help this problem.

• John Frieda Frizz-Ease: the classic anti-frizz product.

• Kiehls Crème with Silk Groom: this product is a favourite with celebrity hair stylists as it conditions and protects whilst you are styling the hair. It controls and defines curls and waves, and smoothes and calms frizz and flyaway hairwhile giving gloss.

I would like to straighten my hair without using irons every day.

• Boots Permanent Home Straightening Kit: this kit is quick and easy to apply, achieving fantastic glossy and straight hair in less than two hours. It tames curls, waves and frizz, giving you the feel of a professional treatment.

My hair needs some TLC as I have not been treating it well.

Try using an extra special shampoo and always use a conditioner.

• Frederic Fekkai RX Protein Shampoo: the Hollywood A list celebrities' favourite shampoo.

• Bumble and Bumble Seaweed Conditioner to hydrate and give shine. Celebrity fan : Gwyneth Paltrow.

My hair is in bad condition from a summer in the sun.

Even if you condition your hair every day you may need a more intensive treatment to help give your hair an extra boost of nourishment.

• Kiehl's Intensive Repairateur Deep Conditioning Pak

• Aussie 3 Minute Miracle Colour Deep Replenishment Treatment

• *Bumble and Bumble Deeep treatment for all hair types. Celebrity fans: Teri Hatcher, Erin O'Connor, Sienna Miller.*

• *Philip Kingsley Elasticizer: a pre-shampoo conditioning treatment to give elasticity, silkiness and strength.*

• *Terax Crema: a cream conditioning treatment used by the Hollywood celebrities.*

• *Frederic Fekkai Protein Rx Reparative Treatment Mask: this strengthens and restores hair that has been overly colour-treated and heat-damaged with styling.*

My hair has lost its shine.
To add gloss you could try using one of the new 'hair gloss' products.

• *John Frieda Luminous Color Glaze: an after-conditioner glaze that creates shine and intensifies colour.*

• *Redken Blonde Glam Crystal Flash*

• *Nicky Clarke Red Carpet Style All A-shimmer Finishing Shine Spray*

I have dandruff.
There are many high street products to help this problem including Head and Shoulders. If you want an extra special one, Phillip Kingsley is a trichologist and his products are excellent.

• *Phillip Kingsley Scalp Tonic*

TIPS

You can use an anti-dandruff shampoo to help speed up the removal of an at-home wash-in semi-permanent new hair colour when you don't like it.

Q: **Does your hairdresser understand you and your hair?**

I always take a picture of the style I would like to show my hairdresser.

If you show your hairdresser a style out of a magazine photographed on a celebrity, the likelihood is that you won't get the look when you next go to wash and dry it yourself, even though the style may have looked good when you left the hairdresser.

When hair is styled on a photo shoot, it is teased and sprayed and fixed to within an inch of its life. You have to consider whether you are a low-maintenance hair woman or are prepared to spend time every day recreating this look. If your hairdresser is worth his salt he will advise you to have a hairstyle that works for your lifestyle, your particular type of hair and also your face shape.

Favourite hair salon

Daniel Hersheson: for haircuts that really work for your face, hair and lifestyle. There are branches in Harvey Nichols and on Conduit Street in London and I have taken many of my celebrity clients there.

I can't create the same hairstyle at home as my hairdresser does.

You won't be able to re-create the same haircut at home as your hairdresser does if it hasn't been cut to work for *your* type of hair. However technically good the haircut is, it still may not work for you. This can be because your hair may be a different texture or thickness.

Points to remember when visiting the hairdresser:

• Your cut should be one that you can manage yourself at home.
• Never put yourself completely in your hairdresser's hands giving him carte blanche.
• Never just say 'cut it' – ask how much he is going to cut!
• Explain exactly what you would like to achieve from your hairstyle in terms of style, manageability etc.
• Be realistic about your face shape, the sort of hair that you *actually* have (straight or curly, thick, thin or fine) when you ask for your new cut.
• Do not sit with your legs crossed when you have your hair cut. You will finish up with a lopsided cut.
• Wear contact lenses, if you often wear both contacts or glasses, so that you can see what is happening.

The neck and hands

These are the two parts of the body that age the fastest and that we tend to ignore. Neck skin is thin with few oil glands so can become quickly dehydrated.

Neck

 How can you maintain your neck's youthfulness?

I do use moisturiser.
Even if you use moisturiser, always wear sunscreen (at least factor 15), and don't forget to include your neck when applying it to your face.

Favourite neck cream products:

• *Elemis Pro-collagen Lifting Treatment Neck and Bust: this has marine algae extracts blended with Royal Jelly and Propolis to help repair, soothe and re-juvenate the neck and décolleté areas.*

• *Clarins Advanced Extra-firming Neck Cream: this helps minimise the appearance of fine lines and firms, smoothes and softens the skin.*

I have a really lined and old looking neck.
If a moisturising cream is still not doing enough for you then you can try a non-surgical treatment to help hold back time on your neck skin tone and lines.

• *Restylane Vital and Elastence: these hyaluronic acid gel fillers can help plump up the skin on the neck. The injections are multiple and the treatment is called mesotherapy. Mesotherapy is the injection into the skin of a gel with active ingredients including vitamins and amino acids. It is said to stimulate the cell restructuring of the skin. You will need at least three treatments.*

• *IPL treatments for sun damage pigmentation. They will also help tighten skin. These are done in courses of treatments.*

- *Glycolic peels will help get rid of fine lines.*

- *Botox can be injected into the neck lines to relax the neck muscles under these lines and soften and smooth out the wrinkles. You will see a subtle change within days.*

- *Isologan can help horizontal lines but may take months.*

- *Collagen facials will include the neck area and can help rejuvenate the skin*

- *Retin-A creams on prescription can also help the neck skin as well as the face.*

(See non-surgical treatments section for more on treatments for anti-ageing.)

Even if you can improve the appearance of the skin on your neck, remember that you can also dress to flatter your neck and body proportions.

Don't wear jewellery around your neck as it will shorten it. Don't wear collars, and if you do, make sure they are small and always worn open. Don't have too much hair surrounding your face and neck.

I have a double chin.
Don't wear necklines that accentuate your chin or stop just short of it, such as a high round neck, as they will only serve to draw attention to your chin. Wide open necks are best for you but you could try to cover and disguise with high necklines such as Chinese style stand-up collars or multi strings of pearls or similar if you have a long neck.

But look carefully at yourself and see which looks better. An open neck or covered up? You may find that drawing the eye away from the neck by showing other flesh is more flattering. Make sure also that there is not too much hair hanging around

6Perfume should be worn wherever you want to be kissed.9

Coco Chanel

Q: So what's your neck like?

My neck is too short.
Wear necklines that are open and deep. This will elongate your neck.

your neck and shoulders as too much hair will make your neck appear worse. A good hairstyle, cut to frame the face and not accentuate the chin, would be good.

If you have a large bust as well as a double chin, then you must show some chest flesh so that you don't appear to have a mono-bosom from neck to torso. A high-necked top will not be a good look for you. But if you were to wear a cleverly designed high necked top that showed the décolleté too, the glimpse of flesh would break up the mono-bosom look.

I have a long neck.
You can wear any neckline as long necks are elegant and swan like. You can also wear any hairstyle up or down.

I don't know which neckline suits me the best.

Halterneck
Can be worn by most shapes except those with extreme shaped shoulders, i.e. not very narrow or very wide shoulders as the halter will make the very narrow look narrower and the very wide look even wider.

Mandarin
This neckline is simple and good for long necks.

Roll neck, turtle neck or polo neck
These necklines are only good for those with long necks and small busts. Never wear high necklines with a large bust. It will make you look larger.

Sweetheart
This fifties style open neckline is flattering to short necks and big busts.

V-neck
This neckline suits most shapes. Widen the 'v' if you have broad shoulders. Lengthen the 'v' if you have a short neck.

Cowl neck
This neckline is good for short necks. It is also good for small busts as it adds extra volume over the bust with the fabric drape.

Slash neck/boat neck
This neckline is open and good for short necks, long necks and to broaden shoulders to balance out body shape.

Frills on the neckline
This is only good for long necks and small busts.

Hands

The signs of ageing are difficult to hide on your hands, so they need to be regularly moisturised and cared for. The skin on your hands is thin and needs extra care and attention. Don't forget about them. It's easy to do so.

Looking after yourself doesn't have to take all day. Even if you don't have time to paint your nails or you don't live a lifestyle that lends itself to painted nails, there is no reason why you can't have clean, tidy, well-manicured hands. Your hands are noticed by everyone, from business colleagues to husbands or partners. There is nothing worse than bitten or dirty nails.

I am the worst culprit for having never looked after my hands over the years. My nails have always been good, but I never used washing-up gloves or hand cream and now it shows. You are never too young to start looking after your hands. The rewards will be there in the shape of smooth skin in later years.

So how can you help your hands look better?

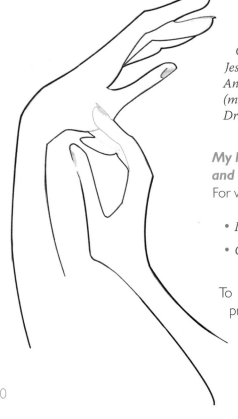

My hands look older than my face.
You can treat your hands to special treatments and TLC when the skin looks tired just as you would your face. Your hands will respond by looking fresher and smoother, just as your face does.

• *Bliss Glamour Gloves: an intensive rehydrating hand treatment. Celebrity fan: Jennifer Lopez.*

• *StriVectin Two-Step Revitalizing System for the hands: this hand care system is a two step hand rejuvenating cream. You apply the first step exfoliant to the damp back of hands, wash off and then apply the moisturising second step. This has made a difference to my hands. Celebrity fans: Jennifer Lopez, Jessica Simpson, Charlize Theron, Anthea Thurner, Val Garland (make-up artist to Sienna Miller and Drew Barrymore).*

My hands have prominent veins and some age spots.
For wrinkles and age spots:

• *IPL treatments*

• *Glycolic peels*

To help plump up skin to disguise prominent veins:

• *Liposculpture or fat transfer. Fat is taken say from your bottom and injected into your hands. This can sometimes make them look lumpy though.*

• *Restylane Vital and Elastence: as recommended for the neck.*

How quickly can I see a difference with the fillers?
You will need to have at least three treatments to see a change.

Will the treatment hurt?
You may experience bruising.

How long will it last?
Around three to four months.

How can I improve my hands with better care?
Keep your nails clean, and all a similar length. Use a daily moisturiser for your skin and give your nails some TLC once a week with a manicure, even if it's only a quick tidy up. There are lots of products out there that are luxurious and pampering for the hands. They don't cost a lot as even the high street chemists have linked up with celebrity nail therapists to create special nail care ranges.

• *Bo'chel by celebrity manicurist Glenis Baptiste for Superdrug. Celebrity fans: Keira Knightley, Angelina Jolie, Gwyneth Paltrow,*

Madonna, Sienna Miller, Kylie Minogue and Kate Moss.

• *Leighton Denny Best Defence Protective Hand and Nail Cream*

What's the best way to do a manicure?

• Using an emery board, file the nails across, gently from underneath, leaving the sides straight. Don't file the sides of the nails inward. You should end up with a gently rounded square shape with the sides not filed away into a slant.
• Massage cuticle softener around the edges of the nail.
• Soak your fingers in warm soapy water.
• Gently push back the cuticle, without cutting it. You can cut the little hang nails away though.
• Massage a good hand cream into your nails and hands. You could use an exfoliator first.
• Wipe away the moisturiser from the nails before painting.
• Apply a base coat.
• Apply the nail varnish.
• Then apply a top coat.
• Finish off with a quick-dry spray or varnish.

NAIL TIPS

What are my essential manicure tools?

- A wooden orange stick with a chiselled end for cleaning under nails
- An emery board
- Cuticle softener
- Nail polish remover
- Varnish, base coat, top coat
- Leighton Denny Quattro Four Sided File and Buffer

My nail varnish always chips and peels instantly.
Essie have a great selection of coloured varnishes that last brilliantly.

What is a classic cool nail colour?

- *Chanel Le Vernis Rouge Noir: the classic quintessential nail varnish colour. Celebrity fan: Kate Moss.*

I always smudge my nail varnish waiting for it to dry.
You can spray your nails with a quick dry spray and be patient.

- *Avon Nail Experts Liquid Freeze Quick Dry Spray*

Or try:

- *Avon Colour Instant Manicure Dry Nail Enamel Strips: this is a brilliant instant manicure which, although slightly fiddly to do, is very effective. There are self-adhesive colour strips that you put on each nail, fold over the nail tip and tear. You remove the colour with polish remover.*

I don't have time to do anything but moisturise.

- *Nivea Age Defying Q10 Plus: with sunfilters to prevent the early signs of ageing.*
- *Nivea Hand SOS Intensive Balm: with vitamin B5 and calendula: for dry and chapped hands.*
- *Sisley Global Anti-age Hand Care*
- *Lancôme Caresse Mains: moisturising and repairing hand cream, with silk glove effect.*
- *Atrixo Regenerating Treatment with vitamin E*

My nails never grow to be very long – they break or chip.

- *Christian Dior Crème Abricot Fortifying Cream for Nails: this restoring nail cream is quite sticky and needs lots of massaging in but makes the nails shine and look healthy once rubbed in.*

❝Everyone thinks I'm glamorous, which makes me laugh because I'm pretty geeky. On Saturday mornings I love watching cartoons in my Care Bear slippers and pyjamas set. How's that for glamour?❞

Mischa Barton

• *Barielle Nail Strengthener Cream: this cult US range was originally created to condition thoroughbred race horse hooves! But now it can give you healthy strong nails too. It has won many beauty awards including CEW USA (2006 Insiders Choice beauty award). Celebrity fans include: Jennifer Lopez, Gwen Stefani, Susan Sarandon, Kate Hudson and Sandra Bullock.*

• *Leighton Denny Skin Like Silk Hand and Nail Scrub: it's a gel that becomes an exfoliant when mixed with water. It moisturises but you can also add a separate moisturiser. Celebrity fans: Jade Jagger, Jemima Khan.*

Body

❝A quick blast of cold water, after a hot shower, does wonders for the skin and circulation.❞

Shirley Bassey

Body cellulite

What don't you like about your body?

I have cellulite and water retention.
You can have cellulite whether you are thin or fat. Your circulation and a sluggish lymphatic system may create water retention. You can try many treatments to help eliminate them but exercise will help most, together with skin brushing and drinking at least two litres of water daily and a healthy diet.

• On dry skin, brush your body every day with a natural bristle brush from your feet upwards towards the heart.
• Have weekly massages if you can afford it or massage yourself.
• Stay away from fizzy drinks, caffeine and alcohol as much as possible.
• Exercise to speed up your metabolism.
• Try to walk or jog at least 40 minutes three times a week.

What spa treatments are there for cellulite?

Endermologie

You are massaged with a roller for at least three treatments a week for around 16 treatments, with occasional treatments thereafter. It really works. I have a cellulite problem and this is what I use when I need help.

My local favourite clinic is Depilex on Wigmore St, London but there are Depilex clinics all around the UK, and endermologie treatments can now be found in clinics all over the world.

Universal contour wrap

You are smeared with a warm mud-style solution and then wrapped with sea clay soaked bandages. You do lose inches. This treatment is great for a pre-party instant fix. You can also buy a do-it-yourself version to do at home.

Rejuva-life

These are pads that are strapped on your body that help you detox, lose weight and tone up. You can drop up to two dress sizes in a month whilst still eating a healthy nutritious diet of three full meals a day.

What can I do to help my cellulite with exercise?

The more you move yourself the better. Your circulation will improve.

Other options in addition to walking, running, exercise classes and the gym are:

Hypoxi Trainer

A thirty minute, three times weekly cycling session with your lower body encased in a low atmospheric pressure egg-shaped pod machine. This increases your metabolism and stimulates the breakdown of fat and toxins. You must drink lots of water during and after, follow a balanced nutritional eating plan, and not have alcohol for eight hours before and after the exercise treatment. The cycling treatments target the waist, hips, thighs and bum, and the Vacunaut running machine targets the midriff and tummy area. The Hypoxi trainer does work. I've been trying it for my thighs and knees. Celebrity fans: Cheryl Tweedy and Ashley Cole.

MBT trainers

Masai Barefoot Technology trainers were designed from the way the Masai warriors walk. They help you tone as you walk, particularly your buttocks. The soles are angled so as you walk you have to become more upright and your muscles are used more efficiently. They are a bit of an acquired taste, although there are those who swear by them.

Power Plate

A vibrating platform on which you exercise and target body areas by holding lunges and poses for a few minutes at a time. This helps to strengthen, tone, improve fitness and flexibility, and eliminate cellulite. Three sessions a week will make a difference. Celebrity fan: Madonna.

What anti-cellulite treatment creams are there?

There are many to choose from and these can help the appearance of the skin by smoothing and firming with regular use, combined with diet and exercise.

• *Lancôme Slim Success Anti-cellulite Attack Serum: this can help make a difference (with twice daily use applied with massage) within seven days and after a month there is a definite difference, especially when used in conjunction with exercise, improved eating habits and drinking lots of water.*

• *Biotherm Celluli-Peel: an intensive peel treatment for dimpled body skin.*

• *Yves Saint Laurent Profil Minceur Non-stop Release Conturing Gel*

• *Elancyl Lipo-reducing Concentrate*

• *SkinGenuity Body Perfecting Formula: this is a gel that can help firm the skin and reduce the appearance of cellulite within two months, with twice daily use.*

• *Sisley Phyto Sculptural*

• *Superdrug Optimum Physique Body Contour Cream: for cellulite/firming skin.*

• *Avon Anew Clinical Lift and Tuck Professional Body Shaper: this cream is Avon's at home alternative to liposuction with 'vacu shape technology' to help firm and lift skin and buttocks in just four weeks.*

Is there anything more I could do?
You can also try a detox.

Elemis Cellutox

This is a whole inner and outer body maintenance programme followed over the course of weeks that you combine with three times a week exercise.

You dry skin brush in the morning, then massage in the Cellutox Active Body concentrate.

In the evening you dry skin brush again. Then you have a bath adding the Cellutox herbal bath synergy. Then you massage in the contouring silhouette cream.

Whilst you give yourself these home spa treatments you also take a course of two types of Elemis Body enhancement capsules, one that helps eliminate the toxins and another that helps the metabolism.

Have you any other suggestions that can help?
Brown legs always look better than pale, so you could use leg-tanning make-up.

Other must have products:

• *A body brush: ideally this should be a long handled natural bristle brush. You should use it daily on dry skin before showering or bathing. It helps exfoliate and also increase circulation, helping eliminate cellulite. The Elemis long handled Body Brush is one of the best brushes, but you can also buy similar at Boots and The Body Shop.*

For tired or heavy feeling legs the best pick me up is this Clarins product:

• *Clarins Energizing Emulsion: you can use this at any time of the day even through stockings to re-energise, refresh and soothe tired legs.*

Hair removal

Maybe in the winter you tend not to bother as much with your hair removal as you do in the summer (as maybe no one will notice), but it is so much nicer to be well-pruned all year

round, even if it's only for *you*. Of course there are those of you who prefer to remain 'au naturel' but I am directing this section at those of you who don't!

I can also guarantee that a 'the only day you didn't shave your legs' dating encounter is likely to happen to everyone who is single as much as a Bridget Jones big pants moment.

In the same way a tidy garden with a mown lawn and trimmed flower beds looks better, so does a tidy and hair free body and you will feel better groomed, sexier and certainly look better in your underwear.

How many times have you had to wear a different outfit, tights or trousers as you hadn't bothered to shave your legs? Celebrities have been 'shamed and shown' in magazines with noticeable under arm hair, including Trinny Woodall of *What Not to Wear* and Julia Roberts.

For the perfect hair removal body care maintenance

You can shave or wax your underarms, legs and bikini line. Waxing lasts around six weeks and is the best solution for the more sensitive areas as the hairs will grow back slowly and not create stubble. Don't wax if you have any rashes or irritations already on the skin.

What do I ask for if I go to a salon for bikini line hair removal?

The terminology for the amounts of hair removed is:

'Brazilian' is a landing strip and 'Hollywood' is everything removed.

I feel embarrassed going to be waxed at a salon.

The therapists see so many bodies all day, just as doctors and nurses do, so there should be no reason for you to be embarrassed. But you can wax yourself in the privacy of your own bathroom too.

• *Boots Smooth Naturally Salon Peel off Wax Treatment: this is a salon-style peel off wax treatment that removes hair without the need for strips. This easy to use system heats inside its own pot. The warm wax helps the hair removal to be quick, easy and effective.*

• *Boots Smooth Naturally Ingrown Hair Minimiser: to prepare the skin for waxing you can start with this nourishing lotion, which gently exfoliates the skin to minimise ingrown hairs effectively and is suitable for use on legs, underarms and bikini.*

• *Boots Smooth Naturally Pre Waxing Liquid Talc: this product dries on contact leaving a thin layer on the skin. When gently massaged, the talc effectively removes excess oil residue to ensure that when applied, the wax can effectively grab each hair.*

• *Boots Smooth Naturally Professional Cold Wax Gel: this sugar-based formula is suitable for even the most sensitive skins.*

Is there anything specific I should do after hair removal treatments?

• Avoid treatments including any heat (saunas, jacuzzis, even hot baths) for 24 hours after waxing or any hair removal treatment.

• Exfoliate and moisturise the skin between waxing treatments to keep your skin soft and smooth.

• Don't tan (sunbathing, sun beds or self-tanning) for 24 hours after waxing.

• Don't use heavily perfumed products on newly waxed areas for at least ten hours after treatment.

I get ingrown hairs.

Once you have been waxed to be as hairless as you are prepared to go, remember to dry skin brush to help prevent ingrown hairs. Also you can use products to help the ingrown hairs from appearing.

• *Medik8 Ingrow Rescue: a professional strength ingrown hair remover to help alleviate and prevent razor bumps, ingrown hairs and shaving rash. Celebrity fans: celebrity make-up artist John Gustafson, Donna Air, Halle Berry, Patsy Palmer.*

I have no time to wax.
Try shaving with a good razor and a shaving mousse.

• *Gillette Venus Vibrance razor. Celebrity fan: Zoë Ball.*

• *Origins Shedonism Sensuous Shaving Mousse*

• *Phillips Bikini Perfect: an electric razor that epilates, trims and shaves.*

Is there anything else I can do?
Laser hair removal is excellent, both for fair and dark skins.

Laser hair removal

IPL treatment can be quite painful and also expensive, but if you can afford it, it's worth every penny. It works very successfully. You shave the areas that are being treated between the appointments that are around every six weeks. You will find the hair growth is reduced dramatically. But you cannot expose these areas to the sun during the course of treatments.
(For more on laser treatments see the non-surgical procedures section.)

Exfoliate

To glow and look radiant like a celebrity, exfoliate and moisturise from head to toe regularly. This will help prevent any ingrown hairs in areas where you have waxed and will also keep your skin smooth and fresh before applying a fake tan. Getting rid of any dead skin will stop the tan becoming patchy and flaky.

You can exfoliate in the shower. Scrubs come in the forms of creams, pastes, oils or soaps that contain exfoliating grains.

• *Lancôme Resurface Microdermabrasion Body Polishing Body Cream: you use this in the shower and it will help 'renew' your skin to look smoother and brighter. It is more effective than a normal exfoliator.*

• *Origins Modern Friction Nature's Gentle Dermabrasion: this is a gentle natural alternative to micro-dermabrasion using rice starch in a creamy buffing paste, to exfoliate, revitalise and cleanse the skin.*

• *ESPA Detoxifying Salt Scrub. Celebrity fan: Helena Christensen.*

• *Caudalie Merlot Friction Scrub*

• *Normandie Keith Lavender Scrub for Tesco: this has a really lovely lavender scent and the oil moisturises whilst the crystals exfoliate.*

• *Lush Buffy soap scrub. Celebrity fan: Kylie Minogue.*

• *Superdrug Natural Firming Body Scrub*

You can also use a cloth to create the same effect.

• *Space NK Japanese Body Wash Cloth: this cloth is great for body cleansing and exfoliation.*

Cleanse

When you shower, wonderful smelling products can make all the difference.

My favourite luxurious ones are any from Jo Malone as they smell so wonderful. You don't really need any perfume afterwards as you will smell so good.

I have sensitive skin.

• *The Body Shop Aloe Gentle Shower Cream*

• *Phyto Soya Soap Free Feminine Wash: especially for sensitive skins.*

Moisturise

My skin is dry.

• *Dr Baumann body Lotion super: contains hyaluronic acid for extra hydration.*

• *Origins Shedonism Deeply Hydrating Butter Cream: for use after the shower or bath. This butter*

cream turns into a luxurious oil for really silky soft skin. The oils and shea butter are combined with exotic smelling sensual fragrances such as jasmine, mandarin, bergamot and basil.

• *The Body Shop Shea Body Butter: a rich moisturiser in a tub for all skin types. Celebrity fans: Jennifer Lopez, Victoria Beckham.*

• *Nivea moisturising range. Products don't always have to be expensive to be effective.*

• *Palmer's Cocoa Butter Formula with vitamin E: all the Palmer's Cocoa Butter moisturising products smell delicious, are inexpensive and can also help smooth rough, dry areas and blemishes. Celebrity fans: Beyoncé Knowles, Diana Ross, Jemma Kidd , Naomi Campbell, Nell McAndrew, Jennifer Lopez.*

• *Tesco Lavender Body Cream with natural essential oil of French lavender*

• *Crème de la Mer Body Lotion: if you can afford this luxurious moisturiser, then go for it! It feels wonderful and is smoothing, soothing and softening . The hydration is long lasting. It can also help fade minor skin discolourations too. Celebrity fan: Halle Berry.*

Are there products specifically to help look after my bust?

• Superdrug Physique Bust Firming Gel-crème

• Clarins Bust Beauty Gel: helps tone and firm. You use this daily first thing in the morning. It's good for the first signs of skin slackening around the bust area.

• Clarins Bust Beauty Lotion: its highly concentrated plant extracts firm and moisturise. You would use this at night in addition to the gel.

• Elemis Pro-collagen Lifting Treatment for Neck and Bust

I have stretch marks.

• Pure Vitamin E Oil

• StriVectin-SD Intensive Concentrate: for existing stretch marks. For maximum results this must be applied three times a day, every day for four to six weeks.

I have severely dry skin and often get eczema. But I would like to try non-steroid creams.

• Botanical Therapeutic Skin Cream Plus for Extra Dry Skin: this cream is one of the best non-steroid anti-inflammatory creams.

• Rio Rosa Mosqueta Oil: you can use this oil for everything from wrinkles to dry skin and itchy patches. It works!

• Cashmere Beauty Rapid Recovery Cream: excellent for severely dry skin and problem skin.

I am pregnant and would like to help prevent the likelihood of stretch marks.

• Ren Monoi Nourishing Body Oil. Celebrity fans: Uma Thurman and Kate Winslet in their pregnancies.

• Palmer's Cocoa Butter Formula Massage Cream for Stretch Marks: with vitamin E, collagen and elastin.

• Palmer's Cocoa Butter Formula Firming Butter: with shea butter, collagen, elastin and vitamin E.

Suntanning and fake tans

Fake tans

You don't have to go on holiday to get a tan as there are so many fake tanning products on the market to get the 'just been away' look. But be careful not to become that 'celebrity orange' hue. Less is always more. Fake tans are now available in all sorts of forms from oils, gels, sprays, and mousses to towelettes.

• Lancôme Flash Bronzer Self-tanning Dry Body Oil: you spray this *over your body and it will give you a golden glow with no smell and dries instantly. Celebrity fans: Robbie Williams, Jessica Simpson.*

• *Clarins Self Tanning Instant Gel: this non-oily gel gives a natural golden tan without the sun and is easily and quickly absorbed when applied.*

• *Estee Lauder Sun Performance Go Tan Sunless Towelettes for Body: these Kleenex sized towels are easy to use especially for self-tan novices.*

• *St Tropez: the full range. Celebrity fan: Cat Deeley.*

How can I make sure I apply the tan evenly?

To avoid orange palms and streaky ankles, you can mix a small amount of moisturiser with the fake tan when applying. The other areas that you can do this to are behind the knees, around the ankles and the elbows, those bony difficult areas.

How can I get rid of streaks?

You can try applying a moisturiser. There are also specific products to address this problem.

• *No 7 Perfect Finish Corrector Wipes*

• *ModelCo Exfoliate Body Wipes: to lighten up colour in over applied self-tanned areas.*

If you want a really even tan you could consider an airbrush tan. You don't have to go to a salon any more to do this as there are now at home ones.

Self tan airbrush sprays

• *Afterglow Spray Tan Professional Home Airbrush System. The make-up artists use this.*

• *California Tan Sunless Spray Gun Kit: gives a natural tan that lasts a week.*

• *Babyliss Beach Bronze Salon Tanning System: you can control the tan density.*

• *Prosun Tanning System: this is easy to use, one of the cheapest on the market and small enough to travel with.*

Suntanning

If you are going away on holiday, then you can start by preparing your body for the sun before you arrive at your destination.

Pre-suntan

• *Lancaster Sun Slim Celluli-Breaker Tan Stimulator: speeds up melanin production to get ready for tanning and also helps firm skin especially in problem areas. You should massage it over your body twice a day at least three weeks before sun exposure.*

Suntan lotion products:

There are so many sun tan lotions to choose from but my favourites include:

• *Liz Earle Sun Shade SPF 15 Body Protector: with antioxidant green tea and pomegranate.*

• *Lancaster SPF 15 Tanning Lotion: my favourite in the top end of the market ranges.*

• *ALL Nivea suntan products are brilliant and work well for all ages and all skin types.*

Tanning moisturisers

Moisturisers will help prolong your holiday tan.

Favourite tanning moisturisers:

• *Lancaster Sunslim Celluli-Drainer Tan Prolonger: contains antioxidants. You massage this over your whole body for at least two weeks after tanning. This cream helps firm and smooth the skin and also maintain the tan for longer.*

• *Nivea Body Sunkissed Skin: my favourite. I use it all summer. This gradually builds up a subtle colour on your skin over days.*

• *Palmer's Cocoa Butter Bronze: with vitamin E and SPF 15. This has a tint you can see when you apply it, dries instantly and smells deliciously of cocoa butter.*

• *Fake Bake Body Butter with Shea Butter*

Tan prolonger/maximer/after sun

• *Lancaster After Sun Tan Maximiser: the Lancaster products all smell wonderful and really do perform as they say they will. This after sun helps keep the skin moisturised and the tan longer without an added fake tan colour.*

Relaxation and healing

However hard you work in your job or at home, you need 'you' time.

This could be taking a long soak in a bath. If you do this it is always nice to add mood enhancing and body moisturising products that work whilst you soak.

• *Dove Regenerating Night Bath: this helps you recoup ready for bedtime and the next day. It has honey in it.*

• *Origins Peace of Mind On-the-spot Relief: you use a couple of dabs of this onto the back of the neck, temples, earlobes and forehead to calm and ease tension. It can also help clear the mind.*

• Aromatherapy Associates Bath and Shower Oil. Celebrity fan: Lisa Butcher.

• Nuxe Huile Prodigieuse

• Ren Moroccan Rose Otto Bath Oil: this luxurious bath oil contains 100 per cent pure plant oils and fragrances. Not only does it smell sensual but its properties will de-stress and moisturise whilst you soak and not leave an oily rim round the bath. It is my favourite bath oil, especially as it is completely natural.

Body skin healers

• Lavender essential oil: you can use this neat on anything from sunburn to insect bites, cuts, sores and spots. It is healing and soothing. It can also help prevent scarring. A few drops in the bath or dabbed onto your temples can also promote relaxation.

• Tea Tree essential oil: you can use this neat on cuts, sores or even cold sores as it is anti-fungal and antiseptic.

Feet

It's as important to look after your feet as your hands. Feet should be regularly moisturised. The hard skin should be removed or pumiced away, the toe nails kept trimmed and clean even if you aren't going to wear polish. Even if you hate your feet, as many women do, you can still make the most of them. You don't have to treat them with disdain. Others who see them may not feel as negatively towards your feet as you do.

Once you have cut your toenails with a good nail clipper and softened and removed cuticles then you should remove hard skin. If you soak your feet first, either in a separate foot soak or whilst in the bath, it will make the skin softer to file. Your toenails will also be softer and easier to cut after a soak.

- *Boots Foot File: for filing away hard skin.*

- *Superdrug Foot Heaven Soothing Foot Soak*

For nails and cuticles:

- *Bastien Gonzalez Unguent for Nails and Cuticles: its essential oils and plant extract nourish and protect the nail and soften the cuticles. Bastien Gonzalez is an A-list celebrity pedicurist who has his own range of luxury pedicure products.*

Once you have given yourself a pedicure then you need to moisturise.

- *Superdrug Foot Heaven Moisturising Foot Butter*

- *Aveda Foot Relief: a soothing cream with lavender and rosemary.*

- *Weleda Foot Balm all natural: with calendula, lavender, rosemary, myrrh and sweet orange.*

❝On the whole, I think women wear too much and are too fussy. You can't see the person for all the clutter.❞

Julie Andrews

• *L'Occitane Shea Butter Foot Cream: lavender scented with shea butter and arnica.*

• *Leighton Denny Sole Pleasure: to moisturise dry or cracked heels.*

I would like to keep my feet smelling and feeling fresher.

• *Scholl Fresh Step Antiperspirant Foot Spray*

My feet always hurt when I wear very high heels.

• *Bastien Gonzalez Silky Talcum Powder: soothes overheated tired soles.*

• *Bastien Gonzalez Sensitive Feet Balm: cools hot feet.*

A celebrity trick for lasting all night in heels is:

Scholl Party Feet: these are gel inserts for wearing inside high-heeled shoes. They cushion the ball of your foot.

Diet and exercise

'You must ask yourself do you like what you see? How do you feel? Are you healthy? Life's too short to have an eating disorder! I like fresh baked bread and cheese too much.'

Nicolette Sheridan

I have worked over many years with celebrities together with top dieticians, personal trainers and nutritionists. I have also been sent to these experts myself so that I can write about what they advise with first-hand knowledge. As a result I have learnt the rules of how to look after myself and others healthily and efficiently. I have also heard from my clients about what problems affect most women.

Everyone needs some exercise and a healthy nutritional diet to feel and look good. Exercise helps your skin, your hair, your digestion, your circulation and also can help fend off the impact of ageing on the whole skeletal and muscular system.

Can I change my shape with diet?

A balanced diet that suits your lifestyle and metabolism will help change your body and your weight if necessary, but not your body shape, however hard you diet.

Diet doesn't mean starvation but eating healthily and in moderation. Don't get too thin. It's ageing. Not only is it ageing, but a curvaceous body is always sexier than a stick thin one. The size zero celebrity culture works in Hollywood, as the camera adds 10 lbs onto your body size and designer red carpet sample dresses borrowed by A-list celebrities are seriously tiny and mostly fit only a size zero. But most of you are not going walk the red carpet

❝I'd rather be a few pounds heavier and enjoy life.❞

Drew Barrymore

or need to borrow a designer sample dress so why not celebrate the body shape and size you currently are? Better fitness and diet will directly change your body by firming and toning it up.

Can I change my shape with exercise?

You will never be able to change your genetic body shape, but with exercise you can define your muscles and sculpt your legs, lift your buttocks and help those under-arm bingo wings.

Toning and firming will instantly help your body shape and you can try to target specific areas with fat-burning exercises. Although those areas will become more toned and therefore appear slimmer with these exercises, you can't actually choose how and from where your weight will disappear. If you are a pear shape you may lose weight from your face and bust first, but you can flatten your stomach and lift your buttocks.

Any aerobic exercise will help raise your metabolism too which will help weight loss without diet. A method that seems to really help target specific areas is the Vacunaut or Hypoxi-trainer (see cellulite section).

Q: **Do you find that the 'slimmer you' got lost somewhere amongst the kids' fish fingers and chips?**

I can't seem to lose the weight even though my kids are now older.

Although you would now like to change yourself, do you feel you are unable to do anything about creating a new you? You need to take control, regain your self-esteem and turn back into that sexy woman that you were pre-children. Yes, you may be older, and body parts not quite as new, but it doesn't mean that you can't look your best.

I will start my exercise regime tomorrow as I have eaten all the wrong things today.

Start your exercise tomorrow but exercise is not something to do as a penance. It should be part of your daily life. It's important to find a type of exercise that you will enjoy doing, otherwise you won't do it. Think positively and if you have eaten all the wrong things today and not done a workout then don't count yourself a failure but just consider it as a temporary blip and start again on the right path.

I am too old to start exercising now.
You are never too old. But if in doubt, check with your doctor first and be aware of your limitations. If you can afford a trainer or advice, even just once to start you off, it would be ideal. Or join a health club or your local leisure centre. Look in your library or on the Internet for classes. Badger a girlfriend to join in with you too on your daily exercise. Even a short slow walk is a start.

I don't have time to exercise.
• Try to get up an hour earlier.
• Substitute exercise for TV.
• Walk to work instead of driving or taking transport.
• Exercise in your lunch hour.
• Divide your exercise hour into two halves and do one 30 minutes session first thing and one before bedtime.

I have never exercised – I don't know how to do it correctly.
However you choose to exercise it is important always to warm up and stretch first. Stretching helps your joints to be slowly acclimatised to the movement to make sure you don't injure yourself and gradually to become more flexible. Warming

up is also very important. This helps raise your body temperature so that you are less likely to injure yourself. Warming up also increases the circulation. Since oxygen is carried in the blood to your muscles, the more efficient your circulation the better your muscles will work. Your heart rate is also speeded up ready for you to be even more energetic.

How often should I exercise?
Everyone should do some exercise daily, even if it's only ten minutes a day. That's better than doing nothing at all. For weight loss you should be doing exercise at least three times a week for 40 minutes a day minimum. The more you do, the more energetic you will feel. Incorporate exercise into your day. Walk up stairs instead of taking the lift. Walk a bit further home from an earlier bus or tube stop, especially if the weather is nice. Try to stand up and sit down without using your hands to help you. This will strengthen your tummy muscles.

Successful exercising is not about beating yourself up with rigorous routines, but being moderate and consistent. Your choice of exercise has to work for *you*.

Don't give yourself impossible goal posts. Take little steps at a time. Even one step on your journey is better than none.

'Find the form of exercise that helps you face stress as well as keeping you fit. Swimming can be hugely calming.'
Shakira Caine

Should I eat before I exercise?
You need energy before you exercise. You cannot have any energy with an empty tum. If you are exercising first thing in the morning how about trying a fruit smoothie or blend some fresh fruits with yoghurt, or even a banana?

When I get depressed I can hardly get myself out of bed let alone do any exercise. I have post-natal depression and cannot motivate myself to do anything.
To help combat depression without medication it has been shown that going out and doing some exercise – even a brisk walk – can help release the serotonin or 'happy' feelings in the brain and make you feel happier and more motivated.

I have to spend at least three hours exercising each day otherwise I will be fat again.
If you have had an eating disorder such as bulimia or anorexia and can only control it by over-exercising to compensate for eating, then you need to try gradually to wean yourself off those extreme hours to no more than an hour and half a day. Try making yourself a chart with reduced

hours. Exercise to this schedule and you will see that reasonable amounts of exercise will be as effective.

I'm embarrassed to go to the gym as I am too fat.
Avoid going to the latest 'cool' gym or classes where you may find that you compare yourself to super fit women who have nothing else to do with their day but work out and look after themselves. Find a course of classes specifically geared to a long term weight loss programme. You will find that there are others like you and it will give you motivation.

I can't run as I have knee joint problems.
It can be just as beneficial to walk. Power walk or walk fast – don't stroll. It's about the energy you put into your exercise. Suitable trainers are very

'What are my glamour tips? Eating well, but not crazily. I never diet. I drink lots of water and exercise.'
Teri Hatcher

important when you have existing injuries. Make sure you stretch at the end of your walk.

I have a bad back.
Posture is very important. If you have a bad back it is very important to support the back itself with the surrounding muscles. So the more you

can strengthen tummy muscles and back muscles the better. When you are exercising, stop before you feel any pain and never do any movements or exercises in a group class that hurt your back. Only do what works for you, not because everyone else is doing it.

If I starve myself for a few days I'll lose weight faster.
Eat regularly and moderately through the day, maybe five small meals. This can regulate your metabolism and keep

I am on a constant on–off diet.
The more you yo-yo with your dietary habits the more you will confuse your metabolism. It will become more sluggish and you will have even less energy. In fact you will become fatter eventually, not thinner.

I get impatient when I diet as I don't lose weight immediately so I give up.
Your current body shape and weight is the result of many months or even years of being that way, so don't give

Everyone goes through a stage where they are not comfortable in their own skin and you have to learn how to be confident and accept yourself. You want to be sexy and have curves, eat whatever you want, because the more you try not to eat, the more you will eat.

Lindsay Lohan

it burning the calories. When you starve yourself by not eating, your metabolism will stop working as efficiently and you will gain weight, not lose it.

I'll start my diet tomorrow.
Don't make excuses. Tomorrow never comes. Today is the first day of the new you, not tomorrow.

up. It needs time to change slowly and adapt to your new healthy living and eating patterns. This will not be overnight or even after a week. It may be a few months before you really start to see a difference.

Do NOT weigh yourself more than once a week. It's all about your body shape and how you look in your clothes, not your weight, as muscle is heavier than fat.

I don't know how to eat healthily.

What you eat affects the whole of you. It is like putting fuel into your car. If you run low on petrol your car doesn't run at all, or if you put the wrong sort of petrol in it doesn't run very well. If you overeat it will be stored as fat. When you exercise you will help burn up the fuel that you fed your body with.

You need carbohydrates, good fats, protein, green vegetables and specific minerals and vitamins (through the food you eat or as a supplement). Ideally you should eat a big breakfast, a smaller lunch and an even smaller dinner keeping all the carbohydrate consumption up to lunchtime.

I eat chocolate and sugary foods to give me energy bursts.

These foods only give you a quick fix energy burst, so that you will have a burst of energy and then slump again. The less sugar you eat, the less you will crave it. To keep you on an even keel, you need to eat foods that are slow energy-release.

Good carbohydrate snacks to give you long term energy rather than a quick fix are ones such as a slice of wholemeal bread, pasta, sweet potatoes, baked potatoes. Even a piece of dark organic chocolate would be better than normal chocolate. If you are really tired why don't you try a taking power nap for 20 minutes? It would be better for you.

Slow energy-release foods include: grainy brown bread (multi-grain, seeded and granary), bran based breakfast cereals, porridge and sugar-reduced muesli, sweet potatoes and boiled new potatoes, pasta with tomato-based sauces, basmati rice and brown basmati rice, grains (bulgur wheat, couscous and quinoa), nuts (no more than a handful a day), fruits (fresh or canned in juice or dried), vegetables (raw, lightly cooked, canned or frozen, though fresh are obviously better, and salad).

Also you may find it beneficial to eat more often, having five small meals at breakfast, mid-morning, lunch, tea, and supper. Keep away from all sugary snacks and refined and processed white flour foods such as sugar-rich breakfast cereals, bread, pizza, pies, cakes, sweet biscuits, doughnuts, croissants and sweets.

'Your body is the direct result of what you eat as well as what you don't eat.'
Gloria Swanson

What are the best foods to eat?

• Beef, lamb, chicken and eggs in moderation
• Fish and shellfish, but especially oily fish such as salmon, sardines, tuna, mackerel
• Dairy including milk, low fat cheeses,

yoghurts (cow, sheep and goat).
• Soya products
• Seeds and legumes
•Nuts (not dry roasted but plain, preferably non-salted)
• Potatoes, sweet potatoes
• Green leafy vegetables
• Salad (lettuce, cucumber, tomatoes, avocadoes, peppers, cress etc)
• Fresh fruit
• Porridge
• Keep to grilling, roasting, boiling or cooking with a little olive oil in a pan

What are the worst?

• White flour, cakes and biscuits and anything sugary
• Chocolate (except dark organic)
• Processed salty foods such as sausages, ham, bacon
• Pre-packaged ready meals, including low sugar/low fat labelled ready meals (because they are mostly overfull of salt and other 'hidden' additives to make them tastier)
• Anything fried
• Anything with too much salt
• Fizzy drinks
• Coffee
• Pizza
• Hamburgers (unless they're home made)
•Never eat carbohydrate laden meal combinations, such as chips with pasta, pizza and chips, or chip butties
•Mayonnaise laden salads such as coleslaw, potato salad
•Sauces such as ketchup, mayonnaise

I keep picking at the wrong things and cheating.
Don't buy these foods for the house. When you shop, make sure that your nibbles are all healthy ones like crunchy vegetables, fruit or even houmous and crispbread, rather than crisps and chocolate. Never do a food shop when you're hungry.

I keep going out to parties and breaking my diet with the canapés.
Eat something proper before you go out, even if you think you might go out to dinner after the party. If you are likely to eat very late, maybe have only a light starter dish at the restaurant and have your 'main course' at home before the party. That way you won't want to pick. Your dress may feel tighter before you go out, but it won't be even tighter the next day.

Q: So why do you eat?

I am unhappy.
You shouldn't comfort eat. Food to help your feelings will only make you feel worse when the sugar 'happy' rush has worn off, as you will regret your binge.

I am tired and need the food to give me energy.
In the same way that the comfort eating will give you a 'happy' rush, it will also

give you instant energy, but energy that isn't longlasting will make you even more tired when it ends.

I am depressed and the food will make me feel better.

Food does not make you feel better. You are the only one who can make you feel better.

I'm fat anyway – what difference will one more day make.

A day will make *all* the difference. If you start today, tomorrow will already be day two on the way to the new you.

I've given up smoking.

You should eat at designated mealtimes, whether it's three or five times a day and take the time to actually sit down and chew, savour and digest your food so your brain and body actually register it was a meal, not a snack. Stop when you're full, don't have seconds and get up and move away from anywhere food related. If you are in a restaurant finish your meal with a herbal tea, not a calorie laden cappuccino.

I am bored.

Don't use food as a diversion tactic to stop doing whatever you don't want to do and don't use food to cheer yourself up – go and do something else for *you* instead.

Because I'm cooking for and feeding the children.

If you are surrounded perpetually by your kids' leftover food or anything leftover you think you might be tempted by, either freeze it straight away into little containers for future usage or chuck it.

I can't lose the weight from my now menopausal midriff.

This is the most difficult part of the body to shift weight from and the area that most women over 40 dislike about themselves. It is difficult to target a specific area of the body to lose weight from but with general weight loss you should find that there is a slight improvement at your midriff. But you can really help tone up an area by concentrating on it with dedicated exercises. And of course there is clever dressing, which we will come to later.

'A minimum of 50 sit-ups three times a week will give you a well toned stomach and one that you will be able to reclaim quickly even after childbirth.'

Jerry Hall

Menopause

❝The really frightening thing about middle-age is the knowledge that you'll grow out of it.❞

Doris Day

This book is not a health manual or health and beauty directory. So with health related subjects like the menopause, I am going to focus more on how to look good than how to deal with the medical aspects.

When you reach the menopause you may experience a slower metabolism, weight gain, loss of skin elasticity, lack of energy, thinning of hair and a duller complexion and sleep disruption. And your weight is most likely to end up around your mid-body and arms.

So I am going to offer some solutions for dietary additions that may help you through your menopause but you should always seek professional help from your doctor or nutritionist too. You could always try an alternative and see if it works for you.

Q: **What foods and supplements can help you through the menopause?**

I don't want to take hormone replacement therapy.

There are many opinions on the pros and cons of taking hormone replacement therapy (HRT), from doubts about its long-term effects to how enthusiasm forwonderful and rejuvenated many women feel when they do take it. There are also natural HRT alternatives. 'Natural' can mean natural as opposed to 'synthetic' hormone replacement and 'natural' as in natural diet and food supplements.

'I have tried taking Dong quai for menopause and a plant gel called Estrogel.'

Shakira Caine

'Anti-ageing clinics' can help you feel good with anti-ageing non-surgical treatments (see section on anti-ageing) and anti-ageing hormone balancing.

What foods and supplements might be beneficial at this time in my life?

Plant oestrogen rich food
• Wholegrains (oats, corn, barley, millet, buckwheat, wild rice, brown rice, wholewheat).

• Soya flour and flax seed oil

• Vegetables

Herbal tablets
• Agnus Castus, Dong Quai, Black Cohoosh, Dong Kwai

Nutritional supplements
• Evening primrose oil

• Essential fatty acids – omega 3 and 6

• Folic acid

• Chromium

• Multi-vitamins

• Vitamin B complex

• Antioxidants (vitamins A, C and E, selenium, zinc, magnesium)

• A herbal sleeping remedy

My skin is so dry.
You should start using richer moisturisers that are specifically created for the mature skin. These don't have to be expensive brands. High street brands such as Nivea and L'Oreal are often just as effective and contain the same ingredients.

Rose and frankincense are two essential oils that are excellent for dry mature skins. Some moisturisers contain these ingredients or you can use them mixed with a carrier oil (see moisturisers section).

I can't sleep.
You could try to have a brisk walk before retiring for the night. Have a hot bath with a few drops of lavender added to promote relaxation. Have a herbal tea such as camomile or a hot drink with warm milk, but not coffee.

'I'm not going to let my hair go grey and walk around with a shopping trolley.'

Julie Christie

I look old suddenly.
It is all probably in your imagination. You are only as old as you feel.

Underwear

Whatever your size, shape or weight, good fitting underwear is all important.

Good underwear together with good posture can make a difference to how your clothes look on you.

'I dress for women, and undress for men.'

Angie Dickinson

Underwear can make you feel sexier and more feminine or just more confident if it is supporting you properly. Corsetry style underwear can create a better body shape underneath difficult dresses, whilst sheer revealing lingerie together with subtle lighting in the bedroom can do wonders to help you feel more sexy and your body look its best.

Having dressed so many celebrities for the red carpet over the years, I've seen how difficult it is to find body shaping underwear that works under red carpet dresses and have created my own website www.redcarpetundies.com for women to buy similar underwear. It includes everything from tit-tape to hold-in pants (as worn by Gwyneth Paltrow after her pregnancies).

'Brevity is the soul of lingerie.'

Dorothy Parker

Q: Does your bra fit perfectly?

I haven't been measured since my twenties. I just guess my size now.
When shopping for your new bra, you should make sure that your breasts sit comfortably in the cups, not overhang the cups creating two extra bosoms. The underwire should not cut in and the straps should not dig into the shoulders. You may need a bigger cup size and a smaller back size for a perfect fit.

The majority of women wear bras that are the wrong size. As you age, your body shape changes. So you will need to make sure that your bra size and fit changes with your body shape.

Where do I go for my bra to be fitted?

The best way to get a bra that fits well is to be measured by an in-store bra fitting expert. But you must find yourself a really experienced fitter as even they too could get your sizing incorrect. It is not an exact science. Even if you think you know your correct size, each manufacturer will have a different interpretation of fit and cut. Department stores such as John Lewis and Debenhams have trained fitters who can advise you, as do Rigby and Peller (who have the 'by royal appointment' coat of arms). This is where I have often taken my clients for fittings over the years, when I advised them that their current bras didn't fit correctly.

For more info on how to fit your bra and sizing chart see:

www.redcarpetundies.com.

My bra felt right when I bought it but I'm not sure any more.

Most high street bras have machine washing instructions and have been tested to be machine washed, but no bra will last as long being machine washed as it will being washed by hand. So you will need to replace your bra more often than you think for it to continue giving a perfect fit. When you buy your bra, fasten it on the loosest hook and then gradually start fastening it on the tighter one as the bra gives and stretches after washing and wearing.

I would like more cleavage.

There are many bras now on the market that have either extra foam padding, or silicone inserts. You can always add extra silicone 'chicken fillet' style inserts for even more cleavage.

My cup size is a DD.
If your breasts are big, it is likely that the best bra for you will have wider straps for support so as not to cut into your shoulders. A good daily wear bra should hold your bosoms comfortably in place without any overspill. Therefore you may find that a higher, less plunging style cup fits you best. If you want cleavage for evening wear, the best fitting bras for bigger girls will have an extra panel in the outer underside of the cup to give a firmer hold and help push the bosoms together. Good fitting bras are all about the technology and infrastructure, not just their appearance.

I have had a mastectomy, but not yet a reconstruction.
Having worked with ladies who have had breast cancer, I know that one of the psychological effects of the illness is the feeling of a loss of femininity with the loss of a breast or breasts. But it's now possible to find sexy masectomy bras and swimwear that have special prosthesis pockets. I don't see why bras should only be functional and not look pretty. It's important for you to feel and look sexy again.

Q: How can you avoid visible pantie line?

I don't want to wear a thong.
Buy your panties at least a size or two larger than your actual size. Even if you hate accepting that you bought such a large size (cut the label out straight away) you will have less visible lines. Other styles that are best for this are 'boy short' style panties and French knickers. Brazilian style panties are half way between a thong and a pantie with a half-brief at the back.

'I don't wear stays. What's the point? If you squeeze it in at one point, it only comes out at the other.'
Lillie Langtry

Don't 'hold-in' pants make the flesh go elsewhere?
If you buy the correct size then there should be no overspill of flesh. Styles that are high-waisted can help too.

I have no bottom, although I am quite a curvaceous larger woman.
'Contour pants' make your bottom more curvaceous like Jennifer Lopez's. They are panties with foam inserts in the two cheek areas that give a naturally shaped curve. You could even wear the pants under your swimsuit if you are that self-conscious about your flat bottom.

Fashion and style

'Fashion is a part of my work. I feel a responsibility to be presentable, to dress up if the occasion calls for it. But really, fashion does not play that big a role in my life these days. The better part of my day is spent in practical clothing.'

Sarah Jessica Parker

Even if your public image is all about glamour it doesn't mean that's how you dress at home. Being stylish doesn't mean dressing up at all times.

Nor does it mean wearing a 'too carefully considered' head to toe combination of current season (or even next season's) brand new designer labels. Maybe this is why the fashion press often criticise Victoria Beckham. To me being stylish means throwing together any combination of clothes (new and old) and still looking great, whatever the outfit or occasion.

An example would be Kate Moss looking as stylish at the Glastonbury pop festival as she does at a black tie gala event. She might not be wearing glamorous evening clothes, but she still stands out from the crowd in her choice and mix of clothes and how she wears them with attitude and confidence.

Stylish women look relaxed, happy and comfortable in both their own skin and their clothes. Older women should be well-groomed and well-maintained, but never look stiff,

'[Style] is an expression of individualism mixed with charisma. Fashion is something that comes after style.'

John Fairchild

whilst younger women can be more adventurous. Clothes can affect your mood, so anything that makes you feel and look fatter, shorter, dumpier, frumpier or older should be removed from your wardrobe. Style is not just about what you wear but how you wear it and how you put it all together. It could be a single accessory that makes all the difference to a simple outfit.

Whatever your size, thin or fat, your body shape is going to determine what you should wear. You should not be unrealistic.

So who is your style icon? Who do you admire? When you dress up, do you dress with her in mind? For example, would you love to dress to be understated like Audrey Hepburn or Grace Kelly? Or do you prefer being more of a trendsetter, like Sienna Miller? Or are you happy just to dress in a style that simply suits you?

So who are *you* and do you have a wardrobe that works for all your life? As a mum on the school run? As a working woman during the day? As a glamorous wife/lover at night?

Dressing well is a perfectly achievable goal. You do not need to have clothes in your wardrobe that are pre-baby (if your children are now grown up) , from your pregnancy, from a previous weight loss or gain, from your last office job that you no longer work in or your last relationship. Even if you own a *classic* little black dress it doesn't mean that it actually still suits you, or that it still looks OK. Your shape may have changed over the years together with fashion shapes.

> ❝*I used to have this horrible style. I had pink and white hair and had this giant papier-mache sea horse that rattled when I'd wear it on my back. Long skirts, eight scarves and bit of plastic...*❞
>
> **Sienna Miller**

In Part One you considered how you feel about your body shape and learnt to focus on the positive, not just the things that you would like to change.

Now you are going to dress cleverly to give the illusion of a more proportional body shape, whatever your size.

Ideally, your shoulders should be roughly in line with your hips (if you were to draw a vertical line from your shoulder to hip).

Your bust should be in the right place and with a good shape (big or small – it doesn't matter).

You should have a waist of some sort, even if it's only *the space* created between your correctly supported bust and your tummy.

There's nothing wrong with womanly curves such as a softly curved tummy and a proper bottom. Most men prefer women with curves.

Legs should appear to be as long and slim as possible.

My style tips

• Less is always more – go for an understated look.

• Understand your body shape and dress for it.

• Be honest with yourself about your size and buy the right one. If it's not the size you want to be, cut the label out.

• You have to be comfortable in your own skin to be comfortable in your clothes.

• Never show cleavage and leg together, just one or the other.

• If you wear a baggy top, team it with a slim bottom.

• If you wear a tight top, team it with a loose fitting bottom.

• Buy clothes to wear that you are comfortable in now, not those that will fit you when you may be thinner next week.

❝I laugh when I end up on the worst-dressed list. I'm not trying to be fashionable. I know I'm kind of a cartoon character. Do people honestly think I'm wearing a kaftan in order to be fashionable?❞

Pamela Anderson

How can you change your body shape with clothes?

You can use specific clothes to create an illusion to balance and flatter. You can use colour, cut and specific style rules to suit and enhance your own body shape.

Using colour

Your body shape will look its best when you consider what colours you need to wear to attract or detract the eye from your best bits and your worst bits. Colour can also make a difference to how you look and feel, and how others see you.

colours to wear that are slimming, such as dark grey, chocolate brown, maroon and navy. Darker colours will help detract the eye whilst lighter ones will attract the eye.

In the same way, shiny fabrics that attract the eye can make you look larger, whilst matte are more flattering.

How shall I wear prints?

Wear prints on the smaller part of you, as a print will make you look bigger than you are. If you choose a print with a darker background it will be more slimming. Wear prints with care; it's better to keep them 'quieter'.

❛The best colour in the world is the one that looks good on you.❜

Coco Chanel

The key classic colours are black, white and camel. Others basic colours include cream, grey, navy blue, brown, pale pink and pale blue pastels.

If you create a wardrobe around basic colours then you need some brighter colours or patterns to give some life, light and shade to your outfit. These are called accent colours.

You can always play safe with a little black dress but there are many other

'Just remember I like terribly simple clothes and I hate prints.'
Jacqueline Kennedy writing to her fashion advisor in 1960

Finding clothes to suit your body shape

The following is a guide to the typical body shapes. I have given celebrity examples wherever possible to help you visualise the shape I am describing, but obviously this isn't an exact science: everyone's body is different and there will be variations within each body shape. Be honest with yourself and try to work out which body shape best describes you, then take this as a starting point for your fashion decisions.

Q: Are you a voluptuous but slim hourglass?

I wear the same size top and bottom. I am slim but curvy with a defined waist and bust and bottom. I want to show off my curves and define my waist.
  Celebrity example: Halle Berry, Liz Hurley.

I feel that everyone talks to my bust when they talk to me.
  Celebrity example: Kelly Brook, Jane Ross (Jonathon Ross's wife).

You are so lucky to have those curves. Most women would love to have a curvaceous shape.

Best shapes for a voluptuous but slim hourglass
• *Tailored clothes*
• *Fitted and shaped jackets to mid hip length*
• *Cross-over and V-necked tops*
• *A skirt that shows off your curves
This could be pencil, seamed, fluted or full-skirted to just beneath the knee*

• Trousers that sit flat on the tum. These could be skinny-legged, baggy or slouchy as long as your top is fitted and it shows you do have a waist
• Dresses that create curves. Good shapes include fifties style with a waist and full skirt, slim and pencil-skirted, wrap, and off the shoulder corset style
• As you are in proportion you can wear smallish patterns

Avoid
• Boxy jackets or tops which hang off your bust
• Straight loose tops, kaftans, tunics, men's shirts, big sweaters, sweatshirts and layers
• Horizontal stripes across your bust or hips
• Large plaid or check patterns
• Pleats over the tummy on skirts, dresses or trousers

Q: Are you a curvaceous, fuller-figured hourglass?

I have a large bust and hips and if I buy clothes to fit my bust and hips, the waist is always too big
Celebrity example: Nigella Lawson and Helen Mirren

Best shapes for a curvaceous fuller-figured hourglass
• Soft fabrics that don't cling or constrict and that don't have too much stiffness or structure. They can be beautifully cut to flatter and skim the body and still not show lumps and bumps

• Simple shapes with no frills or flounces
• Wrap style tops and dresses
• Single-breasted jackets
• Seams, darts and specific tailoring: these make the most of your attributes by drawing attention to your cleavage, waist and curves. The undergarment part of the dress can act like corseting for more defined curves
• Soft and fluid fabrics. Those containing lycra are fantastic, as they are more forgiving on the curves
• Flat-fronted skirts and trousers. Although you may be fuller-figured in the bust and hips, you may be one of the lucky women that have long slim legs. If so, you could wear slim cut trousers

Avoid
• Bias cut dresses as you need definition between the bust and hips and a bias cut dress will not give that
• Double-breasted coats and jackets: they will make you look wider
• Big checks, plaids or patterns
• Tunics, loose tops, straight cut jackets, horizontal stripes
• Trousers that are too loose in the leg: they will make you look bigger

Styles showing some cleavage
• Try layering. You could put a jacket over a shirt over a T-shirt to take the attention away from the hips. The layers can end at various lengths. You could even layer a knee length dress over floppy trousers
• Jackets with a wide collar, lapels, and detailing that broadens your shoulders
• Simple skirts that skim the hips, with panels or in circular fifties style that give movement. Asymmetrical hemline shapes, as they detract from the hips
• Wrap dresses in a fluid, soft fabric
• Empire line (Jane Austen heroine style) waists, but cut without too much fullness over the tummy and hips, otherwise you will look pregnant
• Lighter, brighter colours or patterns are best worn on your top half and dark, plain colours on your bottom half
• Wear heels to help elongate your legs

Q: Are you a triangle or pear shape?

I wear a larger size on my bottom half than my top half and if I put on weight I carry it on my hips and thighs.
   Celebrity examples: Sharon Osbourne, Oprah Winfrey.

I am slim but my hips and bum are bigger than my top half.
   Celebrity examples: Gwyneth Paltrow, Jennifer Lopez, Cynthia Nixon.

Best shapes for a triangle or pear shape
• Clothes that broaden your shoulders to balance out your hips
• Best necklines are wide and open, slash-necked, off the shoulder, wide V, or with wide apart shoulder straps

Avoid
• Halter necks, which draw the eye inwards
• Sleeve seams that are inserted into the arm 'raglan' style. This type of sleeve seam draws the eye inwards, narrowing the shoulders
• Shapeless straight up and down long jackets that fit over your hips but are too big for your bust. They will make you look larger
• Detailing and large pockets on the hips
• Jackets that finish at your widest point
• Skirts or trousers with pleats or gathers

• Straight or pencil skirts that emphasise your hips and thighs
• Eighties style tapered trousers. They will emphasise your hips
• Prints and patterns or designs on your widest parts
• Baggy clothes

 Q: **Are you are an inverted triangle?**

I am slim with broader shoulders than hips and a good bust, but no defined waist.
Celebrity examples: Anna Kournikova, Sharon Davies.

Best shapes for an inverted triangle

• Minimal detailing, simple lines
• Tailored dresses with seams that help the appearance of curves
• Necklines that help minimise the shoulders: halter necks, thin straps, V-necks and asymmetric one-shoulder styles
• Simple single-breasted jackets with narrow or no lapels and little or no padding on the shoulders.
• Fitted or tailored tops with slouchy baggy trousers or cigarette style trousers
• Low-slung belts worn with flat-fronted trousers and skirts that sit slightly lower than your tummy button
• Empire line dresses.
• Baby doll dresses (younger women only)
• A darker colour top teamed with a lighter coloured bottom.

Avoid

• Frills
• Any styles that accentuate the shoulders
• Bias cut dresses that hang from the boobs giving no definition
• Trying to accentuate a non-existent waist. It will only make you look bigger
• Wide belts at the waistline.
• Baggy tops worn with baggy bottoms
• Fifties style full skirts

Best shapes for a lean column

- *You need to create curves where there are none using detailing and cut. Detailing and cut using ruching or stitching can be used to draw attention to your bust. Ruching is simply the gathering of fabric, to add some more volume. Detailing can be how the seams have been sewn together, top stitching or embroidery*
- *Jackets can be tailored or boxy and can have pockets on the hips*
- *Best dress styles are shifts, A-line, high-waisted, Empire line, backless, plunge-neck and long column-style dresses*
- *You are one of the few body shapes that can wear pleats (think men's trouser style) or gathers over the tummy as you have no lumps and bumps*

Avoid

- *Frills and fussy styles. The simpler the better*
- *Close fitting shapes that make you appear even more straight up and down*

Q: **Are you are a lean column?**

I wear the same size top as bottom, have a small bust, a small but non-defined waist and definitely no hips. From the front I look straight up and down, but if I put on weight I do have a bottom.
Celebrity example: Cat Deeley, Nicole Kidman.

I have a boyish shape although I do have a bust.
Celebrity example: Uma Thurman.

Q: **Are you an apple or a rectangular body shape?**

I carry all my weight around my middle and have no waist now. However slim I get, I still have flesh around my midriff but I do have good legs.
Celebrity examples: Joan Collins, Cilla Black, Judy Finnegan.

Best shapes for an apple or rectangle

• Soft fabrics which drape and skim
• Simple, uncluttered clothing
• Wrap tops, with some soft gathered drape
• Necklines should be wide. The more flesh, the more flattering
• Soft-shaped jackets with no collar, or a shawl collar. Never a high round neck
• Cardigan shaped jackets are good as soft lines work best for you
• Skirt styles that are soft and flippy with panels widening toward the hem, or that skim over the tummy or wrap are all good

• Drawstring or flat-fronted trousers work well with slimmish legs
• Colours worn should attract the eye to your face, and bust

Avoid

• Heavy stiff fabrics and sharp tailoring with sharp angles
• Double-breasted or boxy jackets
• Large checks or plaid patterns on top
• High necks
• Three quarter length sleves, as these draw attention to the midriff
• Pockets or detailing anywhere on the tummy or above the hips
• Gathers or pleats at the waist
• Light or bright colour at the waist

Q: Are you petite?

I am only just over five feet tall.
Celebrity examples: Reese Witherspoon, Lucy Liu, Kylie Minogue, Sharon Osbourne (all under 5' 2").

Whether you are a beanpole, curvy, pear-shaped, big-busted or plus sized, if you are petite you MUST dress to suit your proportions as well as your body shape. You will need to consider things like your arm length, body length, and whether you have a short waist or short legs. Try always to buy from petite ranges as the proportions will be correct for you. You will find that sleeve lengths are better and the waists are in the right place.

Best shapes for petite

• You are best in one colour from head to toe to give the appearance of height
• Simple clean shapes that skim the body
• Small accessories and small prints.
• Extra long jeans over high heels
• Shoes that seem invisible in nude or barely there strappy to elongate the leg

Avoid

• Outfits that cut you in half with blocks of colour or wide belts
• Fussy and frilly styles
• Double-breasted jackets
• Anything too baggy worn both on your top and bottom

• Open necklines. You can't go wrong with a wide V-neck shape to balance out your body shape
• Wrap-style dresses and tops
• Corset style tops, which help accentuate your curves
• Marilyn Monroe style plunging halter necks

Avoid

• Any style that draws extra attention to the bust
• Short sleeves that finish at your bust line
• Frills, detailing and pockets at the bust
• Double-breasted shapes as they widen you
• High-necked tops or polo necks as they give you a mono-bosom

❛There's something very awkward about women and their breasts because men look at them so much. Men love them, and I love that.❜

Drew Barrymore

Q: Do you dress to flatter your bust size?

I have a large bust.
Celebrity examples: Salma Hayek, Scarlett Johansson, Drew Barrymore.

Best shapes for a large bust

• Simple shapes and non-patterned fabrics

• Round-necked tops will have the same effect
• Very tight fitted tops, unless you are brave
• Stripes of any kind as your bust will distort them
• Shiny fabrics that attract the eye to your bust
• Bias cut dresses, as you need structure and tailoring under your

bust. Bias cut will fall away under your bust and make you appear even larger
• Black bras under sheer or light-coloured tops

I have a small bust.
Celebrity examples: Gwyneth Paltrow, Calista Flockhart, Kate Moss, Paris Hilton.

You can wear most styles. Small busts do have some advantages.

'What's so beautiful about breasts is their uniqueness. I don't understand the obsession with fakeness. It's a very odd thing, isn't it, to prefer fake and big to small and unique or just beautiful and real.'

Anne Heche

Best shapes for a small bust
• Add detailing such as pockets, buttons, frills, gathers, ruching, beading, patterns to increase the appearance of your bust size
• Wear padded bras and silicone inserts to give extra cleavage
• You can wear plunging, barely there dresses without worrying that everything is hanging out and without the need for a bra to hold everything up. You are very lucky

Avoid
• Stiff structured, tailored clothes that need filling out with curves
• Anything too clingy around your bust

• Tube tops, as they will accentuate your lack of bust
• Low-cut tops that reveal a bony chest

I'm a fuller-figured girl.
Celebrity examples: Queen Latifah, Vanessa Feltz; Fern Britten.

You can show off your cleavage and even your curvaceous bottom with pride, in clothes that flatter. Big women are sexy.

Best shapes for the fuller figure
• Styles that gently skim your shape. You still want to show you have a figure
• Wrap and low V-neck styles work best for your body shape
• If you wear an outfit that you feel is too close fitting then try a sheer looser layer over the outfit to disguise subtly but not hide completely
• You may prefer to always cover your upper arms
• Simple styles work best

Avoid
• Baggy plus-sized fashions
• High necks, round necks and kaftans
• Covering up your body too much, especially at your neck and cleavage
• Shiny fabrics that reflect the light, making you appear larger
• Too many accessories
• Frills
• Boob tubes as they squash and draw the wrong attention to your breasts

Q: Do clothes never fit at your waist?

I am short-waisted.
• Longer style jackets and tops are best. You need to wear a lower waist to cheat the eye into thinking that your body is longer than it is.
• You need to define the area between your bust and waist by wearing a well fitting bra.
• Wear your tops layered and never tucked in.
• Don't wear clothes that have a wide belt at the waist.
• Keep to all one colour, top and bottom. It will help lengthen the torso.
• Wear skirts and jeans that sit beneath the tummy button.
• You can wear low slung belts.
• Patterned skirts can also work for you.

I am long-waisted.
• You need to cheat the eye into thinking that your body is shorter than it is, by bringing the waistline up.
• Break up your torso with blocks of colour. This will help to shorten your body.
• You can wear Empire line dresses or high-waisted styles.

Q: What are your arms like?

I have short arms.
Make sure that your clothes, especially your coats and jackets, have the correct length sleeves. When your sleeves are too long, you can look as though you are wearing someone else's clothing.

I have flabby under-arm bingo wings.
You can accessorise your outfit with shawls, shrugs, wraps, boleros or anything sheer, lace or sequinned that just covers without concealing totally.

Q: Do you have a tum?

I hate my tummy.
You should wear flat-fronted skirts or trousers without pleats or gathers.
You can distract with draped fabric, patterns and belts.

Q: Do you hate your bum?

I'd like to have a more curvaceous bum.
Apparently Penelope Cruz, in her latest movie, had to wear padding to create a larger bum as hers wasn't felt to be curvy enough, as did Jessica Simpson in *The Dukes of Hazard*. Victoria Beckham's bum was digitally re-imaged to look bigger in the advertisements for the Beckhams' perfume. You too could have a curvaceous derriere with 'contour pants'. It's cheaper than plastic surgery!

Apparently there are four types of bottom shape. How can I tell which one I have?

The results of a survey revealed that the ultimate bottom shape is an upside down heart shape, just like Jennifer Lopez's. Other celebrities who have this shape bottom are Kelly Brook and Dita Von Teese, the burlesque stripper.

The three other shapes revealed in the survey are V shaped (wider up toward the hips), square and round.

Very few of us have that perfect bottom, but you should always check out your back view in the mirror to see how it looks in what you are wearing. Many of you may imagine you see a bigger bottom than you really have.

Q: **Do you like your legs?**

I hate my 'tree trunk legs'.
• Never wear skirts that finish above the knee or on the knee. Wear them just below. Wear softer shapes that flow, not tailored styles such as pencil skirts.
• Try wearing soft wrap dresses over soft drawstring or floppy trousers to conceal.
• Never wear patterned or shiny tights, always matte or opaque.
• Never wear shoes with ankle straps, as they shorten the legs.
• Round toes and clumpy heels will make chunky legs look chunkier.
• Choose shoes which are elegant but not too pointy and delicate.

I have days when I feel great and days when my arse won't fit into my jeans and I don't leave the house.

Kate Beckinsale

I have a large bottom with cellulite.
• Keep away from clingy fabrics.
• Never wear smooth shiny fabrics like satin.
• Try hold in pants such as Spanx pants.

I have large thighs.
• Wear clothes that drape and skim, never clingy fabrics.
• Looser boot cut trousers work best to balance out your body shape.

I have short legs.
• Buy trousers and jeans too long and wear them with high heels.
• Wear shoes in natural colours like beige or fawn so that they become an extension of your leg, not a visual point, especially when teamed with a dress or skirt.
• Keep your shoes as low cut in the front as possible. Toe 'cleavage' is sexy and also elongates the foot and leg.

I have long legs.
You can wear skirts and trousers with volume and pattern.

I have skinny legs.
• You can wear textured tights, shiny tights, ribbed tights and opaque tights. Add volume to your legs with baggy trousers.
• Wear lighter-coloured trousers or tights the same colour as you wear on the top half of your body. You can afford to have your legs looking larger and light colours will create that illusion.

I have thin ankles.
You are one of the few that can wear ankle strap shoes and ankle boots.

I have fat ankles.
Never wear ankle straps, or strappy shoes. The more open the better.

Q: **Do you have other dressing dilemmas?**

I am pregnant.
You could either feel really sexy or just really large. If you have never had a bust before and suddenly you have cleavage, why not flaunt it now? Attract the eye to those breasts and detract from the baby bump. Showing skin, especially your décolleté, is sexy.

• Wear off the shoulder tops to show flesh.
• Wrap over style tops and dresses and jersey or soft stretchy fabrics with lycra that hug your body work successfully if you are youthful and have remained toned and fit.
• High-waisted, Empire line dresses with a low-cut neckline will flatter and be sexy.
• Wear jeans with lycra that sit beneath the bump, with slim or loose fit legs.
• Underwear is also important and should be regularly checked for correct size and fit as your pregnancy progresses.

I have just had my baby and I don't look like those celebrity 'Yummy Mummies'.

Very few women are able to spring back into shape like celebrities you see on the pages of the magazines only two weeks after giving birth with a flat tummy and wearing skimpy clothes again. Most women take quite a few months and others years! So be realistic with your post-pregnancy wardrobe. Select an outfit you aim to wear in a month's time. You can always cheat a bit with body shaping underwear like the celebrities do on the red carpet.

Swimsuits to suit your body shape

 How can you look best on the beach however flattering your swimwear?

What can I do to prepare?
You will need to get your body beach-ready. Wax or laser unwanted hair on your legs, underarm and bikini line. Then exfoliate and moisturise ready for your fake tanning session. Make sure your feet look great with painted toenails and no hard skin (see Feet section).

Once you have prepared your body and found that perfect swimsuit or bikini, you need to wear it with confidence, being aware of your posture. You must stand up straight and hold your tummy and bottom in and pull up. Don't stoop to hide your big boobs or tummy. It will only make them look worse.

Wear a sarong or a sheer kaftan over your bikini or swimsuit when you need to walk anywhere. Better to look sexy and confident and covered up to some degree than to feel awkward.

Q: **Do you know which shape of bikini or swimsuit you look best in?**

I have a boyish straight up and down shape.

You, like Cameron Diaz, are the shape that can wear any style of bikini. Try small triangle cups to bandeau tops. If you have no bust you could always try a padded triangle top to add that little bit extra. Bottoms can be 'boy short' style, high cut or tie side.

I have a pear shape.

If you are pear shaped like Jennifer Lopez, Keira Knightley and Gwyneth Paltrow you can wear high legged bikinis that tie at the side, to detract the eye from that area. Padded tops, detailing, ruching and patterns are good to create a bigger bust to balance out hips. Triangular halter necks work well. Just because you feel you have bigger hips or bum doesn't mean that the bikini should be bigger. Sometimes a smaller shaped bikini is more flattering.

I am curvy.

Kelly Brook is the typical curvaceous body that looks best in a bikini that has wider straps for extra support, also giving the appearance of wider shoulders. Wiring and extra support within the frame work of the bra top is important so larger 50's style bikini shapes are best, often with ruching or crossover styles. High cut bikini bottoms are most flattering. Tankinis are also a good option for covering the tum. If you are wearing a swimsuit make sure the back is as low as possible. The higher the back and straighter cut the legs, the less flattering. There is also the 'miraclesuit', a swimsuit with corset control.

I have a large bust.

Even if your boobs aren't Dolly Parton-sized, the better the support in your bikini, the better your figure will look, as big boobs supported in the right place will create a longer torso, and show off your waist. Make sure your bikini has good underwiring and that you fit properly into the cups and don't spill over the top. Halternecks with wide straps are best, never bandeaus.

6I wish I had invented blue jeans. They have expression, modesty, sex appeal, simplicity, all I can hope for in my clothes.9

Yves Saint Laurent

Jeans for your body shape

Jeans are one of the most basic yet essential items in our wardrobe and should work for our body shape whatever size we are. Naturally, nobody can help changing shape, putting on weight or ageing, but by dressing cleverly in the perfect pair of jeans, we can create the illusion of dropping a jeans size even if we actually haven't.

How can the correct fitting jeans really make a difference?

Light will always attract the eye, so make sure all faded or bleached areas are those which you wish the eyes to be attracted to. Fading is always better down the central sections of the jean leg (unless you are slim and wish to look curvier). Pockets and trims will attract the eye so strategic placing of pockets and their design is essential. If you have a small flat bottom, choose a design that has large pockets with detailing. Higher placed pockets will give an instant bottom lift.

I have short legs.

If you are short-legged then wear heels with your jeans. If the boots or shoes are in view then keep them a neutral colour which will help blend into the background.

Prominent vertical stitching down side seams will lengthen legs. Try to avoid too short jeans, cut-offs or turn ups – these create the illusion of shorter legs.

I'm an apple shape.

Apple shapes or anyone who carries weight around their midriff and stomach should look for slimmer cut jeans which show off their legs. If you have great legs you can carry off a narrower leg style. You can hide your midriff with a cleverly cut top, or something looser. But you don't want to wear a loose top and loose jeans – you will look like a shapeless sack! You are one of the few body shapes that can get away with wearing a paler wash or bleached jean together with a darker top to balance out your body shape. This will help to detract the eye from the midriff.

I'm a curvaceous body shape.

Dark coloured boot cut shapes will be most flattering on larger thighs. For larger bottoms, opt for flared boot cut legs as this will help balance out curves. Curvy girls who find that there is always a gap at the waist when the hips fit should wear low-rise jeans which contain some lycra – this will help work with your natural contours.

❛I don't believe in the words fashion faux pas.❜

Christina Aguilera

I'm a straight up and down body shape.

If you have a straight up and down figure with narrow hips, then you can wear most jean shapes, however jeans with structure and heavier denim will work best for you.

To add curves, choose jeans with styling details, pockets and bleaches all in places which will attract the eye and create the illusion of a curvier body shape. If you have a long body, a chunky wide belt will help break up your torso.

I have heavy thighs.

Lycra content in denim has a little more stretch, giving you the chance to find a pair of jeans which fits both your hips as well as your thighs. If you're looking for jeans with roomy thighs and calves, wear styles which don't hug the body, such as a relaxed fit or boy cut or 'boyfriend' jean. Heavier weight denim will help conceal any lumps or bumps.

I have a short body.

If you have a short body and long legs, keep colours as simple as possible so as not to break up the body line. Wear your jeans very low slung as it will make your body appear longer.

I have a large bust.

If you have an ample bust and slim legs you can wear a light coloured jean and dark top to attract the eye away from being top heavy. Wear a fitted top and your jeans slim fitting to create maximum impact.

I am pear shaped.

Wear dark jeans and a light top to balance out your proportions. Make sure the pockets do not draw attention to the hips and wear thinner belts.

Don't forget to look at your back view in the mirror – it's what others will see even if you can't. Designer jeans are usually cut very small and will vary from label to label, so don't be despondent about going up a size. You are more likely to feel bloated the week before your period, so for a 'feel good because you fitted into a size X or Y' moment, don't shop for jeans that week.

To keep your jeans looking their best, wash inside out in cold water to keep the dye colourfast.

'I think better if I have a good hat on...'
Anna Piaggi

Accessories – bags, hats and shoes

Q: **Is the bag you carry correct for your body shape and size?**

The correct accessories complete an outfit stylishly. You can use accessories to discreetly complement and tone in with your clothes like Nicole Kidman and Renée Zellweger. Or you can use scarves, handbags and shoes as style statements, with handbags often the bigger the better, bright coloured shoes and patterned scarves. This may not always be the most stylish look though.

Accessories can completely change the look of the outfit. This season's colours, belts, bags and shoes styles can update something from last season or even vintage from your wardrobe. Wild accessories can jazz up a little black dress. Stylish, beautiful leather bags and shoes can make a simple inexpensive high street dress become part of a chic and expensive looking outfit. Coloured accessories worn near your face can help you look glowing. The wrong accessories can spoil an outfit by making it look cheap, too busy, too young, or too contrived.

'I love Cate Blanchett because she gives everything she wears a personal touch.'
Valentino

I am a larger sized woman.
As with all accessories, larger women need larger sized accessories.

I am a petite sized woman.
Smaller woman, smaller bag.

The reason why women now buy more bags than anything else is because they have that 'feel good' factor. You can be fat or thin and it doesn't matter, as whatever size you are, the bag will still make you feel good when you carry it.

159

Q: **What style hat should you wear for your body shape?**

A rule of thumb would be large woman, bigger hat, petite woman, smaller hat.

How can I balance out my face shape?
A hat should complement your face shape. If you have a longish face, then the hat should have a good deep crown, balancing your face shape, otherwise it will give the appearance of being too flat on the head and make your face appear longer. Asymmetric hats are very flattering to all face shapes. Upward tilting brims help lift and flatter the face to give a more youthful look, especially for the more mature woman.

What height heel should I wear?
If you want to create the impression of longer legs, then go for a higher heel worn with trousers. If your feet hurt wearing high heels try gel inserts such as Scholl Party Feet under the ball of the foot.

Don't wear very high heels with very short skirts and low cut tops. It looks tarty. Flat shoes are of course the most comfortable but do not do anything to help lengthen legs. A ballet style pump is ok, but even a kitten heel is more flattering than a completly flat shoe.

What shape shoe is best for my legs?
Low-fronted shoes are the most flattering to lengthen legs. The more high up the front of the foot, the less flattering the shoe.

> **❝*I'm obsessed with shoes. I must have hundreds of pairs, I'm a shoe fiend – that reminds me I need to go shopping.*❞**
> **Keira Knightley**

Q: **Do your shoes suit you, however much you love them?**

The shoes you wear are very important and can make or break an outfit.

Comfort is paramount and if you have sore feet then you will not be able to relax and enjoy yourself. Standing and walking well can give you the illusion of instantly dropping pounds.

Ankle straps will cut up your leg length, so are only good for very long legs with slim ankles. Few of us have legs like that. Strappy sandals can be flattering as long as the straps are not too heavy.

If you are going to wear sandals, then your feet must be well cared for. There is nothing worse than nice shoes on badly tended feet.

What boot is best for my legs?
Make sure that you don't have any flesh hanging over the top of your boots. The most flattering length boot is one that ends just above the widest part of your calf.

Only wear an ankle boot with a skirt if you have very slim perfect legs like Kate Moss. If you do wear them, team them with opaque tights so they become less obvious. One that sits lower under the ankle is more flattering than one above the ankle. Ankle boots look better under trousers, not with skirts, if you are over 35 or like most of us do not have perfect legs. High flat boots such as a riding boot style look great with full longish skirts. Cowboy boots are fantastic for those of you with bigger calves as they are generous over the calf and work well with full skirts too. Legs too skinny or too wide? Google this and you will find boots solutions on the Internet.

I have wide feet.
If you have wide feet and bigger legs, try a less delicate shoe, not one necessarily with a round toe, but one that has a slightly thicker heel, even a wedge. The lower cut the front of the shoe is, the more flattering it will be for your legs. There are shoes that are made in wider styles. You can find them on the Internet.

I have big feet.
Don't despair. The average model foot size is never less than a British size 7½ or 8, European size 41/42. If your feet are bigger than this then you can find styles to fit you on the Internet and also at a few specialised shops. If you are very conscious of your big feet then don't buy shoes that make a statement. Choose a neutral colour like beige to be less noticeable.

Can I match my shoes with my outfit?
It's always better if you are making a bold statement with colour to not go the whole hog. Less is always more. A red dress is fine but not worn with red shoes too.

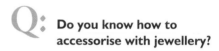 **Do you know how to accessorise with jewellery?**

I would love to wear proper jewellery but can't afford it.
You don't have to be able to afford diamonds to add some 'bling' to your outfits.

It is very easy nowadays to buy a key piece of jewellery that really creates the finishing touch. This jewellery can be cheap and cheerful and from the high street, flea market or car boot sale. It's all about how you wear it. The trick about wearing cheap jewellery is to not pretend that it's real but to wear it with panache. Add more than one strand to make a statement. If it's pearls, make them big and multi-stranded.

161

Are there jewellery rules?

A simple rule of accessorising would be busy dress, plain jewellery; plain dress, busy jewellery.

So what would you wear with a little black dress? You will need to decide if you are going for ladylike, demure and classic or funky with some brightly coloured or interesting quirky jewels. Your choice of jewellery can completely change the look of the dress.

For example, classic elegant jewellery such as pearls will make you look very grown-up. But if you wear quantities of pearls, maybe masses of oversized ones, then you can change the look from classic to interesting and modern. If you take any classic item and wear it in an edgy or unexpected way you will appear younger and more stylish. If you wear a small diamante brooch in a subtle way, as though it were an expensive diamond, it will just look as though you tried, but couldn't afford the real thing. But if you wear it with another brooch/brooches making a statement as a grouping, it will say you meant it to be fun and fake.

Be brave and break the rules with accessories – it's one of the few times that you can.

Your wardrobe

So, let's have a look through your wardrobe. Do you wear all your clothes?

I look in my wardrobe everyday and although I have lots of clothes, I find that I have nothing to wear. It makes no difference whether you have bought your clothes in the high street, your supermarket, a charity shop or a designer store. It's all about whether you actually wear these items and if they really work for your body shape, colouring and lifestyle.

True style is being able to throw together any mix of clothes, making them look great on *you*. It really doesn't matter if they cost a few pounds or hundreds of pounds but it is important that they create the first impression you wish to give off when you are out on a first date, at a job interview, standing at the school gates, with your partner, husband or your girlfriends.

It's not necessary to keep replacing your wardrobe each season unless you are super-rich and live that sort of lifestyle, but it is necessary to check through your wardrobe for clothes that are:

• Too big for you
• Too small for you

- 20 years old, but not stylish enough to be 'vintage'
- Tired and worn
- Stained
- Unfashionable/past their sell-by date.

the sleeve length. Are they both good for you? Do the trousers skim over your body? Does the cut flatter?

Be really truthful to yourself. Step outside yourself and try to see yourself as others would see you. Look at

> **❝People who find fashion strange or trivialising are missing the point. Pride in yourself and the way you look does not convey or cover up any deficiency.❞**
>
> **Baroness Susan Greenfield, scientist**

Q: **So why do you never wear some of your clothes?**

They don't suit me.

By now you should have looked in the mirror to understand your body shape and colouring. You may still see yourself as a different size from your true size and still have self-esteem issues, but you should be able to understand more clearly how to dress for your *best* you.

Try on everything in your wardrobe and imagine that I am there with you, helping you be really critical and even analytical but NOT harsh on yourself. Ask yourself what you feel about this outfit and how you *really* look in it. Ask yourself what is it doing for you. Does it suit your colouring? How is the neckline? Look at your back view. How is it? Look at the length where the skirt hem finishes on your legs and

yourself from all angles. It is important not to forget your back view and profile. You are a three dimensional person and you are seen from all sides. DO NOT just focus on the most disliked part of you such as your tummy. See the whole of you and the positive. Ask yourself truthfully: is it making you look your best?

If the answer is no, then it has to go. You only want a wardrobe full of clothes you actually wear, that work and mix and match together, that suit you and that you really love. It would be better to have a few that you really do wear than masses of clothes that you never wear.

Don't throw these unwanted clothes away, but create piles of them to give to charity, or to sell at your local nearly new clothes shop, on eBay, or at your local car boot sale.

It was a bargain so I bought it.
When you go sales shopping, go with a specific shopping list in mind of what you need to add to your current wardrobe. Either aim to buy wardrobe basics such as a classic coat, trousers or little black dress (LBD), or make a list of the gaps in your wardrobe. Do you need a perfect pair of black trousers? Do you have a top that goes with your favourite skirt? Do you have a dress that you never wear because you don't have any shoes that go with it?

Only buy what you really need. Do not buy that must-have bargain, even if it was £2000 reduced to £20! A bargain isn't a bargain if it doesn't suit you, fit you or work in your wardrobe. And don't buy it with the thought that you'll wear it when you lose weight. Live in the moment and buy it to wear now. When you shop, wear appropriate underwear that will work under the intended outfit (for example a plunge evening bra if you are shopping for an evening dress) and take a pair of heels to try things on with.

I thought I liked it but I don't think it suits me.
Now that you are aware of what works for you, your body shape and colouring, you can be more discerning about your past wardrobe choices. Did you buy a dress because you thought it was a pretty style? But does the colour really work for your skin tones? Did you buy a sweater only because the colour went with your favourite trousers? But does the sweater have a polo neck that makes you look larger, as you now know that you look better in a V-neck? Have you looked at your back view in that pencil skirt? Are you seeing cellulite as the fabric is too sheer? Is that shirt straining at the buttons over your bosom? Is the neckline of the T-shirt you wear all the time the wrong shape for you? Do you keep buying baby pink items when actually you look better in a shade of coral pink?

Imagine I am there asking you all these sorts of questions and be ruthless with your clothes. Remember this is the beginning of the new you.

A woman's dress should be like a barbed wire fence. Serving its purpose without obstructing the view.

Sophia Loren

I bought it out of desperation.
Do you always wait to shop for that outfit you need for tomorrow at the last minute? Is this because you are waiting to lose weight and hate how you look at the moment? Do you feel embarrassed about how you look in the mirror and feel that you will be judged by the shop assistants? Do you think you won't find anything suitable in your size? Do you not know how and where to start? Or do you hate shopping? If lack of money is your problem you can shop at places like Primark where you can pick up the latest looks for only a few pounds.

If you are shopping for a last minute outfit, be focused and have in mind the look you would like to achieve, even if you are not happy with your current body shape. It's about making the best of yourself now – not in the future. Is there something in your wardrobe already existing that you can update with new accessories – new shoes, bag, belt or jewellery? Does it need altering, adding new buttons, new zip, shortening, lengthening, taking in, letting out, repairing or dry-cleaning?

It was a spur of the moment purchase.
Most boutiques and stores will take your purchases back within 28 days and give you a refund as long as you have your receipt and the clothes are pristine and unworn. So if you get it home and realise that it really doesn't make you

look your best for any reason, take it back. You don't have to explain – just say it is unsuitable. The retailers are not going to love me for reminding you of your rights but much better that you don't waste your money on clothes that are only going to hang unworn in your wardrobe.

It's too big for me now.
So you have lost weight and lots of your clothes are hanging off you. Some can be altered at your local dry cleaners but others will be too complicated to start playing around with as it may cost more to alter and re-make than to buy again new. Once you start altering some styles, the proportions become out of sync.

Check the fit. Do the shoulders hang off your shoulders? It is essential that these fit correctly. Do you need to bring in the shoulder seams? Can you take in with darts or extra seams? If you take in the waist band of a skirt or trouser what is the impact of the alteration on the fit around your bottom? Consider all these things before you commission the alteration, as how ever good it is, it may completely change the look and the original styling of the item.

It's too small for me now.
If you really are certain that you are going to get into this item of clothing again one day not in the too distant future, then I will allow you to put it

on the top shelf for the celebratory day you reach your target weight… But does it actually suit you when and if it fits again? Is the colour good for you? Is it something that works with the rest of your wardrobe? Do you need it? There is a difference between want and need.

I don't feel comfortable in it.
Comfortable doesn't only mean how something fits – too loose or tight – but how you feel in it. Do you feel uncomfortable because the neck is low and you think you may be exposing too much cleavage? Do you worry about your back view? Do you hate your knees or calves and the dress finishes just in the wrong place? Maybe subconsciously you know the colour or pattern doesn't suit you so you feel uncomfortable.

To look and feel great in your clothes you must feel comfortable inside and out. On the inside, because it's how you feel – confident and maybe even sexy in your outfit. On the outside, because it's how you look – you know it works for your colouring and body shape and suits you.

I thought I'd keep it for sentimental reasons.
Are you too old to wear it now? Could the outfit make you mutton dressed as lamb? Is it old fashioned rather than something that you could bring out again to wear as 'vintage'? It is always nice to keep clothes for sentimental reasons, whether it is to pass down to your children, grandchildren or just to have for a memory, but if you are keeping it to wear again, then look at it and then at yourself and see if the two still match.

My partner or husband bought it for me.
If your partner or husband really cares and understands you, he should welcome the fact that you are re-evaluating the inner and outer you, as the likelihood is that not only you will benefit but so will he and your relationship together. So if you feel bad that he bought it for you and now you are getting rid of it, then explain why it doesn't suit you any longer so that he will understand and buy you something next time that suits you and that you feel sexy and wonderful in when you are out together.

❝I try to mix ladylike sweetness with really sexy vampiness.❞

Jennifer Lopez

It's too sexy for me.

Do you want to wear clothes that make you invisible and that do not draw any attention to you?

Do you feel that if you wear a low neckline showing some cleavage, it becomes too sexy and that you feel underdressed, over-exposed and maybe appear in others' eyes to look 'tarty'?

If you are wearing a dress that reveals some cleavage, it is best not to show leg at the same time, especially when you are of a certain age, however good your legs are.

But if you have a good bust, why not show a little of it off? It will attract the eye and detract from all the other bits of you that you dislike.

Maybe you grew up having a larger bust than your school friends and became conscious at an early age of how breasts become the focus of unwanted attention from men, and how eye contact in conversation hovers there rather than on your face. So now you want to cover them up. A hint of cleavage won't automatically attract men's eyes. You body shape will look better too with some flesh on show.

I don't feel sexy in it.

Sometimes classic styles can make you look old before your time. Avoid blouses with bows, boxy suits, tweeds and anything that's too severe. A classic style can be made to look more sexy with colour added as an accessory. Flash a bit of lingerie lace – just a glimpse. Mix something unexpected with a classic – maybe even a denim jean jacket over a silk dress to dress it down. And of course you can always wear a pair of sexy shoes.

I keep putting it on but never wear it as I don't feel right in it.

Is it the colour that is too pale, too dark or the wrong hue against your skin? Or is it the cut that doesn't work well for your body shape? If you have an item of clothing that has hung in your wardrobe unworn, get rid of it. Replace it with something that works.

You should not have to try on lots of outfits that are discarded across the bedroom before going out every day or evening.

'I leave notes saying I apologise for the state of the closet. I'll clean it up.'
Sarah Jessica Parker

I don't have anything to go with it. Try it on and decide what style, shape and colour you need to buy to team with this item. When you go shopping take it with you so that you can colour match it and also see if everything works together. Sometimes something that looks good in the shop doesn't really work how you thought it would when you get home. It might be also that the sales assistant was very enthusiastic and persuasive.

Wardrobe tips

Treat your clothes with care and they will last better. It doesn't matter whether they are cheap or expensive but give them the same attention.

* Always air your clothes after wearing.
* Check your clothes for stains and wash or clean if necessary after wearing *before* putting them back in the wardrobe
* Iron them before putting them away in your wardrobe. That way you'll always have something to wear in the morning
* Check for fallen hems, missing buttons
* Don't wear the same pair of shoes every day. Rotate them so that they get aired and don't smell
* Clean your shoes and mend worn down heels
* Hang your clothes on non-wire hangers so the clothes keep their shape

Shopping tips

* Make your wardrobe shopping a battle plan, not a whim
* Make a list of what you really *need*, not *want*
* Make a list of what you have in your wardrobe that needs something to go with it
* Make a list of what items need accessories, belts, shoes, jewellery, cardigans
* Do you already have the wardrobe basics? Such as great black trousers, LBD, white shirt, jacket, skirt, day dress, evening dress, evening cover up
* Only buy what you can fit into now. Not if or when but today
* Only buy a jacket if it does up. Don't say, 'I'll wear it open.'
* Don't buy a top only to wear under something. Each item needs to be able to stand alone
* Don't shop when you've been for a long boozy lunch

- Check that you can return the item if not suitable as long as it's unworn.
- Wear comfortable shoes to shop in and take a pair of heels to try on with.
- Wear underwear that supports well and works under evening wear as well as day wear.
- If a dress or jacket needs more than three areas of alteration, don't buy it.

Dressing appropriately for an occasion

The job interview

I don't know what to wear.
You have 30 seconds to create that crucial first impression. Find out exactly what employees are likely to wear in the workplace of the job you are going up for. If it is a casual younger style workplace, you could find the approach to dressing more casual, with jeans and T-shirts being the norm, or no dress code at all, whereas in a professional situation where the men wear suits and ties you will need to dress in a similar vein as there is likely to be a dress code. Dress as though you are already working in the company.

I haven't got anything suitable.
You don't have to wear a suit to look professional. You could team soft unstructured separates such as cardigans or wrap over cardigan style jackets with skirts or trousers. Clean, tidy and groomed is the most important. Clothes that look tired, dirty or unkempt with buttons off or hems falling down and faded areas are not appropriate. Make sure your shoes are clean and polished and your heels are not worn down. Trainers are generally not suitable.

I am too fat to get in my old work clothes now.
I would suggest looking for an outfit that fits you well now, with a soft shape and layering. Wear a top that covers your tummy, with an unstructured jacket or cardigan over it and a soft line skirt. A pair of medium height heels, not flats. Although structured tailoring flatters most figure shapes, office work wear has now evolved to softer tailoring and separates. A good handbag is important.

The new job

How can I dress to look my best at work?
How *you* look influences your client's view of the company. Dress appropriately, especially if you have client meetings. It's not just about dressing appropriately but also good grooming. You should have a stylish

haircut, or at least clean and tidy hair. Wear some make-up so that you look as though you take care of your appearance and make sure that your nails are clean and not too long.

I would still like my personality to show.
Corporate dressing doesn't have to be boring. Interesting accessories add the finishing touches to all outfits. Even a watch can say volumes about you (see accessories section).

Can I wear skirts or dresses?
Try mixing and matching jackets and skirts. A jacket and skirt can look as smart as a suit, while a dress can look business-like and elegant too. A dress with a crisp fabric and tailoring such as a belted shirt-dress would be better than a wrap dress. Plain or patterned but floral is a little too girly. If you choose to wear a cardigan rather than a jacket, keep it elegant and go for fine-knit in cotton, cashmere or lambswool, not chunky.

I don't want to look too sexy.
Don't wear shapeless clothing to disguise that you are female to your male colleagues. You can still look feminine without flaunting it. Wear clothes that skim the body, not cling, and that flatter your shape, without being revealing. It's all about being appropriate.

Excess flesh is not appropriate in the workplace. Being feminine is good, but not being provocative. Cleavage, spaghetti string tops, visible bra straps, bras showing through sheer tops, crop tops, holiday shorts, micro miniskirts and leggings are all inappropriate, as are beach style flip-flops, even in the heat of the summer.

For winter, choose fabrics that are lightweight wools and wool crêpes. In summer, choose crisp cottons and mixes, not linens, so that you don't look as though you've slept in your clothes. Avoid thin flimsy fabrics that have no weight or substance.

Working at home

I work from home.
Try to get dressed each day, out of your tracky bottoms or pyjamas. Even if it's only into jeans and a T-shirt. It will make you feel more motivated.

Casual

What does 'casual' on a party invitation mean?
Dress to look good in daytime clothes, not party clothes. Maybe smart jeans teamed with a crisp white shirt, or

trousers and an interesting top. It's not the time for stilettos and sexy dresses.

Smart business casual

If I am asked to wear 'smart business casual', what does it mean?

Smart business casual means wearing the sort of clothes that you would expect to meet someone in, who works in a similar profession to you. An outfit that is appropriate to the brand you work for and your job position. The impression you give off must say you are above all professional and authoritative, you know what you are doing, you are efficient and also well-groomed.

Smart casual

What does 'smart casual' on an invite mean?

Simple but elegant. Not jeans, shorts, or anything you'd wear on a day to day basis or for work. You need to look as though you've made an effort. For daytime, it could be a dress, a beautifully cut pair of trousers and a top. Linen works well for summer, although it creases, or crisp white cotton, which you could mix and match with some colour.

For evening, again you could wear a dress, even a little black dress or the wrap dress that works for all body shapes. Anything in silk is always a good classic wardrobe staple. Any fabric that is sensual to the touch will look more elegant. Shoes should be elegant and a high heel makes an outfit more evening.

The dinner party invite

I don't want to be underdressed – but equally don't want to be overdressed.

• Do you know what any of the other guests are wearing?
• Ask the hostess or a friend who is going what she is wearing.
• Mix understated with glam such as silk or lace top with jeans.
• Dress down a cocktail style dress with something more low-key such as a suede or denim jean style jacket.
• Accessorise up a simple little dress (you can always sneak off to the loo to remove the accessories).

The cocktail party

The invite didn't have a dress code suggested. I have no idea what to wear.

If you wear something classic you can never go wrong, or look out of place. Don't go down the jeans and evening top route. You don't know how dressed up the other women there may be. You can't go wrong with a well-cut pair of trousers or a skirt and an evening top in silk, chiffon, or with a bit of sparkle. If you hate your arms wear a sleeveless top that might show some cleavage covered with a cardigan or shrug that is sheer and beaded or sequinned. The little black dress is always the safe option. Cocktail party style is sexy but elegant, feminine and ladylike.

The black tie event

Black tie no longer means that a long dress is a must. A knee length or longer cocktail dress can be appropriate too. It is also very chic to wear a beautifully cut female version of the tuxedo suit teamed with very high sexy heels, and a lace or silk camisole underneath.

You can then check what they are wearing, if you prefer to be part of the crowd. If you want to stand out, wear a colour, as so many wear black, but do consider whether you want all eyes on you or not.

I can't afford a new dress.
Black tie doesn't have to mean a new dress but it does mean *dress up*. Dressing up means looking glamorous, elegant and sexy. Even if you have worn the same dress before, you could change the look of it with different jewellery, accessories and shoes. You could even change some of the trimmings on the dress if there are any. No one will ever notice, especially if you look wonderful in it. They'll only notice you looking your best. If you feel

❝ I hate stealing the show, but I'd worn a lot of black, covering up things, and I thought – not this year. ❞

Kate Winslet when she wore the red Ben de Lisi dress at the Oscars

However, men will always find a dress sexier. But be comfortable in what you wear. You will have a miserable evening if your shoes are too high and your dress too tight. Remember you will also need to sit down and eat at some point in the evening. It's always worth doing a phone around to other women you know who are invited.

good in a dress why not wear it again. Lots of celebrities recycle their clothes, especially old favourites.

'The only rule is don't be boring and dress cute wherever you go. Life is too short to blend in.'

Paris Hilton

Any model or Hollywood actress who wears fancy designer ball gowns knows how to expertly manipulate gaffer tape to mush, lift and hold your breasts like a bra. It's a perfect temporary boob job. When you wear those complicated, low-cut dresses, and you're 40, that's how you can achieve perfect cleavage.

Teri Hatcher

How can I find underwear to make the most of my figure under my clinging revealing dress?

To look sexy in your long dress, remember how to dress for your body shape and make the most of your curves, attracting the eye to the bits you like and detracting from those you don't. If you have great legs, find a long dress with a slit on the leg. If you have good shoulders, go for a one shouldered Grecian style or strapless. And of course you could always wear a backless dress. But don't forget to wear lingerie that holds you in, up and gives your body a great shape underneath the dress. Having dressed so many celebrities for the red carpet, I realised that some never owned a suitable bra or the stylist's essential double-sided tape themselves.

I am worried about my outfit.

Before you leave home and you have decided on your outfit, check yourself in front of the mirror. Does the dress fit? Is your underwear hidden? Is your dress revealing too much when you lean forward or walk or just move? Do you need tit-tape (double-sided tape) to stick the revealing parts of your dress to your body as the celebrities do for the red carpet? Or do you need control pants to hold those lumps and bumps in?

'I like to move fast, and wearing high heels was tough, and low heels with a skirt is unattractive. So pants took over.'

Katharine Hepburn

❛The key to looking good is inner happiness, calm and confidence.❜

Fiona Fullerton

I am not very good at walking in heels as I usually wear flats.
Are your shoes new or have you road-tested them before? Can you actually last an evening in them without serious pain? Comfortable feet equal a great night. If they are very high, try Scholl party feet gel inserts for under the balls of your feet. Too high is not good. Better to be comfortable and be able to walk with confidence and ease than totter, especially after a few drinks.

I would like to look glamorous.
Glamour is about really *owning* your look. It's about feeling drop dead gorgeous, and feeling and looking sexy. You don't have to be wearing a revealing dress that lets it all hang out – it could even be chic and black – but the dress always has to be worn with confidence, great posture and attitude. Glamour gets noticed; you cannot be invisible if you are glamorous. Glamour catches the eye. It shows off your curves. It makes other women jealous.

Always dress for you. If you feel good then you will look good to others.

Part Three
Being Your Best You

How you can make the
most of the new you:
the third stage and final
part of your journey

By now you should have asked yourself questions and found the answers. You will have looked in the mirror and seen yourself as others see you and should be looking at a brand new reflection of yourself. One that is more confident and optimistic.

You've soul searched in Part One of your journey, and learnt tricks to improve the physical you in Part Two. Part Three is all about putting yourself out there in your 'new you' mind and body and seeing who appears.

You are now aware of how to make the best of your face and body shape with clothes, beauty products and quick fixes. You may not have implemented any changes yet, but you are ready to do so. The most important thing is being in the mindset to make those changes. You should no longer be putting off the exercise and maybe diet regimes until another day.

You approach everything now with a positive attitude. If you are happy in your own skin, and more accepting, you will exude energy and optimism. You don't have to change your face or your body, all you have to change is how you see yourself. You are now standing at the crossroads of your new life and need confidence to go out and get.

So how are you going to really change your life? What are you going to do about getting out again, creating new relationships and maybe a new social circle of friends? How are you going to start having a more vibrant social life, a new job and working life? These are the final elements of discovering the new you.

'Anyone's life truly lived consists of work, sunshine, exercise, soap, plenty of fresh air, and a happy contented spirit.'

Lillie Langtry

So how are you going to kick-start your new social life? Is your life like being on the treadmill? Can you never find time to get out of your home or your office? If you really want to change your life, it's important to find a balance between your daytime 'job' – everything from being a mum and doing the housework and chores to whatever paid daytime job you may have – and your 'you' time.

Your 'you' time could include getting out to exercise, even if it's only a short walk, taking up a hobby, getting out to a place where you can socialise with friends or make new ones. You need an activity that is only for *you*.

So where do you go for your 'you' time and how do you make new friends?

Work out your priorities and the people you *really* want to be with. Health should be your number one priority, family the second, and friends the third.

> **'You time' suggestions**
>
> • Try voluntary work. Helping others always makes you feel good. Try www.csv.org.uk; www.timebank.org.uk.
> • Go for a walk.
> • Try learning a new sport.
> • Try learning a new skill.
> • Delegate some more at work.
> • Pamper yourself. Try essential oils in the bath or go for a massage.

Real enthusiasm comes from the heart and ignites the whole system. If you have that, there's no resistance, nothing to sabotage your actions. You can succeed at almost anything.

Anita Roddick

What celebrities do for their 'Me time'

Kate Winslet

'I love a night at home in front of the telly. I'm in that dressing gown and love it. I'm all for comfort and being cosy.'

Shakira Caine

'I swim religiously. Every day if possible. When things get too much, when I feel I can't cope, I swim for an hour. It's important to find out what *you* can do to relieve stress, and how to cope with it.'

Sandra Bullock

'On my ranch in Texas I can recharge my batteries and revel in doing absolutely nothing, just watch the grass grow, enjoy the sunset and see friends.'

Mary Nightingale

'Pruning and digging in my garden gives me the greatest feeling of relaxation and calm. 'I get a real sense of satisfaction when I see the results of my hard work. A sunny afternoon with the secateurs and a large spade – heaven!'

Demi Moore

'I like being physical and being out and about. I spend a lot of time going to the park, the zoo or the beach with the kids and taking bike rides.'

Joanna Lumley

'Deal with stress by breaking anxieties down into small manageable areas. Always give yourself rewards, like a nice cup of coffee, during a stressful day.'

Making new friends

❝I refuse to join any club that would have me as a member.❞

Groucho Marx

I don't know where to start.
You need to get out of the house to meet new people. Whether you live in the town or the countryside there will always be somewhere that is the heart and soul of your local community.

How do I begin?
If you live out of town, and you don't know anyone else in the area, you need to take up an activity where you will meet other men and women. Obviously in a big city there will be more choice as you only have to look in your local paper, the library or in the window of the newsagent to find out what's happening locally to you. And of course there is the Internet to search on. If you live in the countryside, there may only be the village post office but that is where you will hear all the local gossip and what's happening where.

So where are you going to go? And what activity would you now like to learn?

Tips on places to make new friends

- Health club
- Exercise class
- Tennis club
- Dancing classes
- Cooking class
- Art class
- Bridge club
- Starbucks coffee shops
- Art galleries
- Weight watchers
- Local evening classes of any sort

I'm shy.

Are you too shy to go out on your own and join a class? Do you think that others will be judging you or is it because you won't know anyone? But the others may not know anyone either. So have a go and imagine everyone else to be as shy as you. Look out for someone else who is standing on their own and be brave and strike up a conversation with them. They will be eternally grateful to you, as they may have even less confidence than you. A brave face often covers huge insecurities.

Did you always want to learn to paint or play bridge? Now's your chance.

There is a myriad of classes in which you could enrol and meet other like-minded women.

If you live in town, the world is your oyster for places to go and things to do and you will be spoilt for choice. But although there are so many choices, it doesn't mean that anyone is actually going to talk to you there. So you need to choose carefully an activity that involves interaction with your fellow classmates in pairs or groups. It could be as sedentary or energetic as you please. It's not really about the activity. It's more about meeting and mixing with new groups of people.

You could always have a regular skinny latte at your local coffee shop. Drink in – not take out. You may find that there are interesting regular visitors there too.

So you've now joined a club and are going out and about to new activities, but you find that you are still not really able to relate to people properly.

❛Think sexy and confident. It all starts in the head.❜

Ivana Trump

Is it your body language that is putting them off? Why do some people manage to attract others to them like moths to a light and others stand on their own, even if they are good looking?

What is charisma?

The word charisma is from the ancient Greek word *kharis*, meaning gift, as if you were seen to be charismatic, the Gods had breathed a special gift of the spirit into you. So how do you become charismatic? It's about having a magnetism and aura that compels you to be noticed. There is no reason why you can't develop from being an introverted person to an extroverted one.

There is a difference between just 'being present' in a room, feeding off others' energy, and creating your own energy source which will draw others to you. It's about being an upbeat and confident person, with body language to match. It's about the attitude you present to the world.

Men and women who have charisma use eye contact to engage with you. This indicates that you are the 'chosen one' and that they find you fascinating. This makes you feel good as all focus is on you. A person you find yourself attracted to and liking after a conversation will leave you in a 'feel good' state as they gave you their undivided attention. Successful charmers have positivity and are skilled at expressing and transmitting these positive emotions to others.

But don't you have to be really pretty?

A charismatic person isn't necessarily the best looking but one who generates a magnetic energy source. The power of attraction is about fooling others into thinking that you are the most interesting, gorgeous person in the room. This is not about twiddling hair strands or getting out that cleavage but drawing people into your aura. Be intriguing and charismatic and attentive to your admirers. Make them think that you are the best listener in the world and nothing matters at that moment other than what they are telling you. Even if it is absolute rubbish!

'We all lose our looks eventually. Better develop your character and interest in life... Character contributes to beauty. It fortifies a woman as her youth fades. A mode of conduct, a standard of courage, discipline, fortitude, and integrity can do a great deal to make a woman beautiful.'
Jacqueline Bisset

How can I become charismatic?

• Accept yourself and your faults. This makes others feel comfortable with you as they can identify with your faults too. No one's perfect.

❝When I was 25 I was so lacking in self-esteem that I didn't have the confidence to enjoy my fame or shine socially. I never felt able to really let myself go, because I was so worried what the man would think.❞

Fiona Fullerton

• Try to relax and be at ease; it will make others feel at ease too. Try to hide your tensions and stress.
• Be open to meeting new people and always with a positive attitude. Be interested in them. You may be pleasantly surprised.
• Smile. It changes others' attitude to you.
• Be optimistic, a 'glass half full' person. You will find that this is infectious. Others are drawn to the confident, optimistic person, not the shy and frightened individual slouching in the corner.

• Be calm. Don't forget to breathe and if you find yourself breathing very fast, try to take some deep breaths to slow your breathing down.

Your body language tells all about you to others. You can use it to show others how you feel and to read how others react to you. So if you are shy, lacking in confidence and have low-self esteem, over-ride these thoughts and think about the physical you that is being shown to the world.

❝Men's traditional view of sexiness isn't sexy– it shouldn't be so obvious. Push-up bras and miniskirts? Sexiness to me is when people are comfortable with themselves.❞

Sienna Miller

Making a good first impression

"Accept your age and the wisdom it brings."

Joan Collins

How can I make a good first impression?

- Don't smile nervously and automatically at everyone you meet. Be slower with your smiles and make the person you are meeting aware that your smile is fully intended just for them. Make them feel special.
- Encourage the people you are meeting to talk about themselves. Pay attention and wait for them to finish their answers.
- The best way for getting people to talk is 'reciprocal disclosure'. Reveal something about yourself and the other person is likely to respond with a similar disclosure.

- Concentrate and don't look distracted and over their shoulder.
- Try to match and emulate the pace and volume of speech of your companion.
- Don't be hostile or argumentative.
- Be aware of how people react to you. Do you still have a connection or are they avoiding eye contact or looking bored? If so, why? Are you talking too fast, or is it all about you?
- Don't invade the other person's personal space.
- Everyone has something to offer. *Especially you*. So don't try too hard to be liked, but try to be more open to liking others and you will find others warming more to you.

I feel self-conscious when I walk into a party.

How are you walking into a room? Do you walk with a confidence and assuredness, holding yourself tall? Conjure up an imaginary friend at the end of the room, preferably near the bar and walk purposefully towards this area where you can stop and collect yourself again. Even if you didn't need a drink it gave you a reason to walk in that direction too. Once you have your drink you can scan the room to see who you might know or who you'd like to get to know. Your outer shell of confidence will bring others to talk to you, whilst you stand there. Always look happy and upbeat. A miserable looking person will be ignored.

I feel self-conscious when I am meeting someone new.

Are you standing with your arms crossed or leaving them loose at your sides? Crossing your arms creates a protection around you, a barrier. You should appear open and friendly, not closed and wary. When you are meeting someone for the first time, do you sit in a relaxed and attentive way or in a frightened and defensive way? You may not even realise that you are doing this. You will often find that you are mirroring the person whom you are relating to. You may find that you are both sitting in the same way and doing the same things with your arms. You will certainly find this happening if you are flirting. But it can happen everywhere, even at a job interview.

I need to appear confident at my job interview.

Eye contact and openness are very important when you are being interviewed. As an interviewee, you will not get on well if you are perceived to be hiding something by never looking your prospective boss in the face. Remember to sit with your legs crossed if wearing a skirt.

It doesn't matter how good you may be at your job or look in your interview clothes if you don't have the correct body language at the interview. Don't invade the interviewer's personal space. Don't be manic with your gesticulations or enthusiasm, and don't cross your arms as this can be perceived as defensive. You may also find that you mirror your interviewer's body language you could seem too relaxed. Sit up and be poised and collected.

Dating and relationships

‘Always be more important than your clothes.’

Paris Hilton

Q: What impression do you want to give on your first date?

I want to appear sexy but not too sexy. How should I dress?

• Your date wants to go on a night out with *you,* not your outfit. Make sure that your outfit is appropriate for the person you are meeting and the location.

• Don't go for too sexy, too skimpy, too short, too much cleavage, too tight. In fact 'too' anything is out. (Men want to look at other women wearing too little– not the one that they are with, in case everyone else is looking at her for that reason.)

• A man wants to be proud of the date that he is out with – not embarrassed. If you are wearing something with some cleavage revealed, cover up the rest. You could always reveal your shoulders or back. They can be just as sexy.

• Don't wear anything that you need to constantly adjust or fiddle with.

• You want to look uncontrived, as though you threw the outfit together (stylishly), even if you really took three days agonising over what to wear.

• A skirt or a dress will make you feel more feminine.

• If you're really not a dress person, then go for a sexy evening style top teamed with jeans.

• And if you want to feel sexy without dressing to be obvious, then just wear some sexy undies.

I would like to look like the woman he'd want to marry.

This is not just about what you are wearing but how you conduct yourself. If you really want to be with this man, then you have to be *you.* So is the 'you' that you are showing

❝When I'm alone, I can sleep crossways in bed without an argument.❞

Zsa Zsa Gabor

this man the real one? Or is it an act? No one can sustain the act of being someone they aren't for any length of time. And if you do, you are not being true to yourself or to your prospective partner. A good relationship is based on truth.

I don't know how to look self-confident.
It's all about body language. How you hold yourself. How you walk, hold your head up, use your hands and gestures and how you stand. Think about being tall and proud. Try to have your facial expressions, arms and hands as relaxed as possible.

I have forgotten how to flirt.
Have you forgotten how to flirt, or do you flirt with everyone, even your own sex? Flirting is fun and can attract admirers to you. Flirting is all about body language and eye contact.

Do you make eye contact, or do you studiously avoid catching anyone's eye? Eyes tell you everything about how you feel… happy, sad, lonely, excited, sexy or scared. This is also why if you fancy someone, you look into their eyes. If you do want to start up a dialogue or a flirtation, you do so by engaging eye contact, even across a room. Some people are scared of eye contact but others may feel that if you are prepared to look them back in the eye you are honest and up front and confident.

How can I seduce him into thinking I'm wonderful?
To charm is to seduce and you can seduce not only for sex, but to 'lure' others into your 'friendship fold'. If you have created a scenario where you have charmed someone into feeling at ease with you, then you may also have created a feeling of intimacy and warmth. Flattery, eye contact, light flirtation and making someone feel good about themselves are the keys. A good example of this is Jonathon Ross, who draws his guests into his aura by flirting harmlessly with them.

Q: Can you work on and improve your existing relationship?

Maybe you already have a partner with whom you are dissatisfied, and the relationship is less than perfect.

I grew up with the idea that there would be my perfect man somewhere.

Are your expectations in love too high? Did you grow up with the notion that you would meet your knight in shining armour who would whisk you away on his white charger into the sunset and then you would both live happily ever after?

If you are expecting too much, and no one is perfect, what happens when the initial rush of passion wears off and cracks appear? Do you try to fix them or just keep moving on to the next relationship and only staying around whilst it is still perfect? You may find that each relationship goes the same way after the initial passion fades.

But you could break this cycle. Be more tolerant of each other. Everyone is human. Try to understand your partner's way of thinking and try to keep the romance alive. Find time for each other and talk. Just because you have a partner doesn't mean that you have to live in each others' pockets.

Keep some life of your own too. Every relationship needs to retain a little bit of mystery and a few harmless secrets.

Q: Are you now dating second time around?

A new relationship will make me feel better.

When you are looking for a new relationship, for that 'perfect' person to appear on the horizon, are you expecting this exciting new relationship to make you feel better about yourself?

A new relationship will not fix your problems. It may bring excitement and passion into your life, but it will not change how you feel about yourself and how you relate to others. To have a strong and well-balanced relationship with another person, you must love yourself first and then he/she will love you.

You cannot search for approval from another to endorse and uplift your own self-esteem.

It's also not necessary to give up yourself to love someone else. You have to love and respect yourself first and foremost before you can give to someone else.

You never know when you might meet someone. If you look they don't come. New relationships happen in the most unexpected circumstances. Also, potential new lovers appear rather like buses. None at all or all at once.

You may find once you are happily dating someone, others appear more interested too. Maybe when you are in demand you no longer look or appear as needy or possibly even desperate (even though you may have been unaware of this).

I am single and find the idea of dating again very scary.
It's all about being proactive , You are never going to meet someone staying in watching the TV in your pyjamas. Cultivate your friendships with your single friends so you have someone to go out with. It's never too late to start afresh. There are many ways to start looking, from meeting friends of friends in your own circle to bars, singles events and online dating, which no longer has a social stigma.

I'm too old to start dating again.
You are never too old to start dating. You are as old as you feel. Look at Kim Cattrall, Teri Hatcher, Demi Moore, Sharon Stone. Yes you say, they are all more successful, rich and beautiful. Of course they will have their own issues about getting older, but it's all about self-belief and confidence, whatever your age. I believe that there is someone for everyone, and that 'someone' appears when the time is right. As life moves on so do your needs. But you need to feel good about yourself and happy with yourself before you find someone else you can be happy with.

My next relationship will be my final serious long term one leading to marriage.
Don't put so much pressure on yourself or your partner. Why don't you take this relationship day by day and see where it goes? You have much more chance of success and you won't frighten him off.

Why would anyone want me?
Because you're worth it. Just because someone else didn't want you, doesn't mean that no one else will. Be yourself. You will attract others by the 'signals' you send out – positive body language together with how you dress and look. Acting or looking desperate, miserable or needy will not attract others – it will send them away.

❛A bit of lusting after someone does wonders for the skin.❜

Liz Hurley

'My husband makes me feel very loved which gives me confidence. I know that affects how I look.'

Liv Tyler

 Q: **Do you always go for the wrong man?**

I go for a man who is needy.
Don't make yourself feel wanted by trying to rescue or look after someone else, look after yourself first.

I go for the bad boys.
Ask yourself what you are gaining from these relationships. Do you live your life off an adrenalin rush and only want passion and excitement? Calm down and look at what you really want from a long term relationship.

'I stayed in relationships that weren't right too long. I've since understood that, but I'm still very loyal.'

Linda Evans

I choose boyfriends who bully me and treat me with disrespect and violence.
Don't feel that you are worthless and that it must be you that is causing them to act like this. Stop taking the blame. Don't keep forgiving them. Move on and find someone who treats you like a queen. You are worth it.

 Q: **Do you think you could feel sexy again?**

'Being a sex symbol has to do with attitude, not looks. Most men think it's looks, most women know otherwise.'

Kathleen Turner

What makes you feel sexy? Is it something you wear (clothes or perfume), or something that someone says or does? Or have you forgotten what feeling sexy is? Feeling sexy is a state of mind and once you feel sexy you will look sexy.

It's about feeling self-confident and knowing that you look your best. If you feel gorgeous then that's how you'll look. If you feel good on the inside you will look good on the outside. Feeling sexy gives you a different walk and a stance with attitude.

Learn to trust your mirror. Don't rely on others to tell you how you look and for compliments and endorsements. Accept what you see in the mirror and appreciate you. Tell yourself how great your hair is, or that you look sexy in a dress. Don't be negative and see a couple of extra pounds you think you may have put on over the last few days. Re-affirm the positive.

Q: How can you enhance your sex appeal?

I am not sure that I have any.
Everyone has sex appeal, but some have more of it than others and some know how to work it. Sex appeal doesn't disappear as you get older. In fact, it can become stronger with maturity and self-confidence. Sex appeal is not about what you are wearing, or even *not* wearing. It's about what you give off. But you have to feel confident in yourself to feel sexy. This is why we all love the naughty men who have a twinkle in the eye. They exude confidence and give off the message that they can have anyone they want.

Q: Have you met your new man and are at the beginning stages of your relationship but want to make sure you don't make the same mistakes as you have done before?

I don't know whether to tell him the truth or play games.
There is no beating about the bush with later love as the need to appear cool seems to disappear in your forties and beyond. Also, there isn't a minute to waste! Life isn't a rehearsal. Directness can only be a better base from which to start a relationship as you know where you stand.

A man will never be able to read your mind. Don't play games. Be honest with each other. But maybe don't put all your cards on the table straight away and possibly be busy (or pretend to be) at least one night of the week!

I may be frightening him off.
Do you wait for him to call you or are you texting him before you even get home after the initial meeting? Are you so predatory that you are frightening him off? However much you may be lusting after a man, let him pursue you and feel like the hunter, not the prey.

'It's true that sex gets better with age.- you stop comparing yourself to other people. You just have to relax and be yourself.'

Janet Ellis

Tips for making a relationship work

• Try always being affectionate and don't be afraid to kiss or hold his hand unexpectedly
• Make sure you always communicate
• Say what you really feel and don't hide your feelings
• Be true to yourself and to him.
• Be honest
• Listen to what he has to say
• Understand him
• Laugh together
• Be kind
• No one is perfect. Don't expect him to be

❛I'm the kind of person who couldn't care less about sex until I meet someone who I think is wonderful. I sort of feel sorry for the next man who gets me. I may just have to kill him with passion.❜

Kirstie Alley

Q: **So are you ready for sex with a new partner?**

How long should I wait before I have sex with my new man? How many dates?

'The longer you wait before you have sex the better. As my grandmother used to say: why buy the whole cake if you can get a slice free?'

Joan Collins

There is no exact answer to this although I have asked so many of my male friends their views.

There is the 'first date' theory. Men don't marry girls who sleep with them on the first date.

And there is the 'third date' theory: three dates are enough time to get to know each other, enough to know that you want to take the relationship that stage further. Also you aren't just dragging it out and wasting his time, or yours (even if the dinners are nice), as

neither of you is just looking for another 'friend'.

It's often the men nowadays that wish to wait longer than you to commit to sex. Roles have reversed. If something feels right for both of you – why not? But sex on a whim can lead to feelings of love for a person who is entirely wrong for you. Are you repeating a pattern of attraction to the wrong men?

I feel strange having a new boyfriend to stay in my home with my children.

This is a dilemma that happens to all single mothers at some time. If your children are small I would suggest that that no one stays over and meets them in the morning until you really know that this boyfriend may become a serious fixture in your life. If your children are old enough to have had their own adult relationships and understand, then it is really important to discuss how you all feel about a new man sleeping for the first time in your bed after their dad.

Communication is all. You may find that they only want you to be happy rather than being shocked that you now have a new partner and therefore a sex life.

The thought of sex with anyone new after all these years fills me with horror.
A good relationship both in your everyday life and in the bedroom is all about communication. Communicate your fears and thoughts and if your new partner loves you, he will listen to you and be understanding.

comes with age and maturity rather than your perfect body. If he just wanted that he could date someone his own age.

As you should now be in the 'new you' frame of mind, you should have started to tone up your body with a healthy diet and exercise and feel good about yourself, or at least more confident. You can always conceal and disguise those bits that you really can't change with soft lighting and well-fitting sexy underwear. You'd be surprised at what men do and don't notice.

The best lovers do not necessarily have the best bodies. Your partner is not in bed with your cellulite or your stretch marks, he is in bed with *you*.

Sex is God's joke on human beings.
Bette Davis

I'm worried about someone new seeing me naked.
Childbirth and weight gain and loss together with time and gravity may have taken the toll on your body, but your new partner should be wanting you and loving you for who you are, and the whole of you, not being super critical about you. If he is likely to be that critical then he is not the one for you.

If you happen to be dallying with a much younger man, he will have been attracted to you by your self-assurance, knowledge and sexual confidence that

Being comfortable and confident in your own skin, being able to laugh and being loving and giving will be far more appealing than a perfect body. Let your partner know whatever he is doing makes you feel wonderful and everything else will be forgotten.

'I married the first man I ever kissed.
When I tell my children that they just
about throw up.'
Barbara Bush

'You can love more than one person in your life, but things will be different. There'll be a different dynamic. Needs and desires change.'

Francesca Annis

How will I know what to do after all these years of abstinence?

You will know. It's like riding a bicycle. You never forget.

My last partner told me that I was no good in bed.

When you sleep with your new partner, It's very likely that you will find out that maybe it was your last partner who was no good. Not *you* at all.

I love my partner but it's not just about sex to me.

Everyone requires something different from their relationships. Some people need passion, others hot sex.

The best and longest lasting relationships work because you are both each other's best friend. But don't let all the hugs and kisses stop too, as all human beings need some physical contact.

❛*You know you truly have intimacy when you can totally be yourself.*❜

Joan Collins

Tips to remember for the 'new you'

I always wanted to be somebody, but now I realize I should have been more specific.

Lily Tomlin

• Focus on one thing at a time. Then you won't feel dragged in too many directions.

• Make a small list of 'to do' tasks for each day. Not too large. The list needs to be manageable. Tick them off as you do them and feel success when you look at the ticks at the end of the day.

• Don't feel guilty saying no. You don't have to please everybody all the time.

• Don't waste time on getting wound up about small things. Put things into perspective.

• Allow others to help you, even if you don't think they'll do it as well as you.

• Make time for *you*.

• Drop 'if' and 'tomorrow' from your vocabulary.

• Stop criticising yourself.

• Stop judging yourself.

• Stop worrying what others think.

• Say sorry if you're wrong.

• Smile.

A small change can do a lot. And when you find things improving for you, accept and embrace them and be happy.

Now that we have taken this journey together, I hope that you are on the road to being that 'new you' you never imagined you could be.

Never forget that you are unique, have special qualities and always have something interesting to contribute and bring to a partnership, friendship or a social occasion. Don't be too harsh on yourself, undervalue yourself or put yourself down. You deserve to treat yourself and be treated as someone special.

Even if it takes you another year or even two to achieve your final destination of weight loss, learning a new skill to start a new career, or just making some new friends, you are on the right road.

You now know all the ways to make yourself look and feel your best even if you don't implement them all at once. It's always about one step at a time. A little baby step, not a big leap.

Every so often you will come across an obstacle, a 'red traffic light' or even a diversion which will hold up your progress, but these things happen. Everyone is human. It doesn't mean that you have to give up. Just pick yourself up and start again. Always look forward, never backward.

'A woman is like a tea bag. It's only when she's in hot water that you realise how strong she is.'

Nancy Reagan

Accept yourself for you who are now, not who you were. Allow yourself to change as you continue with your journey. Your view of the world and how the world views you will evolve along the way.

Good luck on the rest of your journey.

We are all on a continuous one, just at different stages of it. Discovering your best you is all about you being the master of your own destiny. Don't leave it up to others. Create your own destiny.

Resources

Aculight • 0870 900 5959 • www.aculight.co.uk
Afterglow • 0844 800 0128 • www.afterglowspraytan.com
Amazonia Preciosa • 0870 4460 210 • www.realce.co.uk
Aromatherapy associates • 0208 569 7030 • www.aromatherapyassociates.com
Asda • www.asda.com
Atrixo • available nationwide
Aussie colour mate shampoos • available nationwide
Aveda • 0870 034 2380
Avon • 0845 601 4040 • www.avonshop.co.uk
Babyliss • 0870 513 3191 • www.babyliss.co.uk
Barielle • 0208 740 2085 • www.barielle.co.uk/www.spacenk.com
Bastien Gonzalez • 0208 740 2085 • www.bastiengonzalez.com
Benefit • 0901 113 001 • www.benefitcosmetics.com
Bioforce • 0800 037 1020 • www.bioforce.co.uk
Bliss • www.blisslondon.co.uk
Bourjois • available nationwide www.bourjois.com
The Body Shop • 01903 844544 • www.bodyshop.co.uk
Boots • 0845 070 8090 • www.boots.com
Botanical therapeutic cream • 0800 389 8195 • www.victoriahealth.com
Botox • www.botox.com
Bumble and Bumble • 0207 836 0818 • www.windlehair.com
Burts Bees • 08456 049 049 or available from John Lewis
California Tan • 0800 587 2583
Cashmere beauty • 0207 952 7681 • www.cashmerebeauty.com
Caudalie • 0800 44 292 424 • www.caudalie.com/www.spaceNK.co.uk
Chanel • 0207 493 3836 • www.chanel.co.uk
Chantecaille • 0208 740 2085 • www.spaceNK.com
Christian Dior • 0207 216 0216 • www.dior.com
Clarins • 0800 036 3558 • www.clarins.com
Clinique • 0870 034 2566 • www.clinique.co.uk
Cover FX • www.coverfx.com
Cover Girl • www.covergirl.com
Crème de la Mer • 0870 034 2566

Daniel Hersheson • 0207 434 1747/0207 201 8797 • www.danielhersheson.com
DCL Europe • 0207 467 8462
Depilex, Wigmore St. • 0207 486 0852 • www.depilex.co.uk
Dermagenetics • 01737 700 020 • www.dermagenetics.com
Dermalogica • 0800 591 818 • www.dermalogica.co.uk
Dove • 0800 085 1548 • www.campaignforrealbeauty.co.uk
Dr Baumann • 0845 833 5505
Dr Brandt • www.spaceNK.com
Dr Cecilia Tregear • www.wimpoleskincare.com
Dr Denesse • 0870 190 0003
D. R. Harris and Co • 0207 930 3915
Dr Hauschka • 01386 792 642 • www.drhauschka.co.uk
Dr N. V. Perricone MD • www.nvperriconemd.co.uk
Du Wop • 0208 740 2085 • www.spacenk.com
Elemis • 01278 727 830 • www.elemis.com
Elizabeth Arden • available nationwide • www.elizabetharden.com
Elnett • available nationwide
Endermologie • 0208 731 5678 • www.lpgsystems.com
Eporex • 0207 226 6560
Espa • 01252 741 600 • espaonline.com
Essie • 0208 906 9090
Estee Lauder • 0870 034 2566 • www.esteelauder.co.uk
Eucerin • www.eucerin.co.uk
Eve Lom • www.evelom.com/www.space nk.com
Eyelure • 0208 573 9907
Fake Bake • 0870 054 4455
Frederic Fekkai • 0208 740 2085 • www.spaceNK.com
Freeze 24.7 • www.spaceNK.com
Fudge • 0800 515 906 • www.fudge.com
Galvanic spa II • 0800 093 2359
Ghd • 0845 330 1133 • www.ghdhair.com
Guerlain • 01932 233 887 • www.guerlain.com
HB Health • www.HBHealth.com
Hylexin • 0870 837 7377/Selfridges • www.hylexin.com
Hypoxi Trainer • 0800 731 1323 /0870 414 6969 • www.vacunaut.co.uk
Imedeen • 0870 1188 070 • www.imedeen.co.uk
Jane Iredale • 0208 450 7111 • www.janeiredale.com

Janina • www.janina.co.uk
Jeff+Maggie • 0845 330 3330
Jemma Kidd • www.jemmakidd.com
Jo Malone • 0207 720 0202 • www.jomalone.co.uk
John Frieda • 0207 851 9800 • www.johnfrieda.co.uk
Joico Joigel • 0800 515 906 • www.joico.com
Hope • www.planetblueshop.com
Kiehl's • 0207 240 2411
Kerastase • 0800 316 4400
L'Oreal • 0845 399 1949
L'Occitane • 0207 907 0301
La Prairie • 0870 160 7270
Lancaster • 0870 160 7270
Lancôme • www.lancome.co.uk
Laura Mercier • 0208 740 2085 • www.lauramercier.com/www.spaceNK.com
Leighton Denny • 0845 004 2053 • www.leightondenny.com
Licorice Balm • 0871 871 9975 • www.skinshop.co.uk
Liz Earle • 01983 813 913 • www.lizearle.com
Lush • 01202 668 545•www.lush.com
MAC • 0207 534 9222 • www.maccosmetics.co.uk
Mason Pearson • www.hqhair.com
Marks and Spencer • 0845 302 1234 • www.marksandspencer.com
Max Factor • www.maxfactor.com
MBT trainer • 0207 684 4633
Medik8 • 0845 673 2222 • www.medik8.com
MD Skincare • 0208 740 2085 • www.spaceNK.com
ModelCo • 0208 740 2085 • www.spaceNK.com
Mop • 01282 613 413
NARS • 0870 837 8377/Selfridges
Natralox • www.natralox.co.uk/www.redcarpetundies.com
Nicky Clarke • 0800 0853 848
Nivea • www.nivea.co.uk
Nuxe • 0800 316 3164
Olay • www.olay.co.uk
Organic Apoteke • 01234 757 744
Organic Pharmacy • 0207 351 2232 • www.theorganicpharmacy.com
Origins • 0870 034 2566 • www.origins.co.uk

Palmer's • 0208 554 7000
Philosophy • 0870 990 8452
Philip Kingsley • 0207 629 4050 • www.philipkingsleyproducts.com
Phyto Soya • 0208 763 1414
Pout • 0207 379 0379 • www.pout.co.uk
Power Plate • www.power-plateuk.com
Prescriptives • 0870 034 2566
Pro-ferm by Vitalize • 0208 740 2085 • www.vitalizehealth.com
Prosun • www.ukhairdressers.com
Redken • 0800 444 880
Rejuva-Life • 01372 844 674 • www.rejuva-life.com
Remington • 0800 212 438 • www.remington.co.uk
Ren • 0845 22 55 600 • www.renskincare.com
Restylane • 0800 015 5548
Rosa Mosqueta Oil • www.nutricentre.com/www.redcarpetundies.com
Rose and Co • www.hqhair.com
Ruby and Millie • 08450 70 80 90
Scholl • 0800 074 2040 • www.schollpartyfeet.co.uk
Shu Uemura • 0207 235 2375/0207 235 2375
Simple • www.simple.co.uk
SK-11 • 0800 072 1771
Sin Ecch arnica • www.alpinepharm.com
Sisley • 0207 591 6380
Skingenuity • 0870 067 3396 • www.physonics.com
Skinindulgence • aboutfaceuk@uwclub.net
Sovage • 0207 235 5000/Harvey Nichols
St Tropez • 0115 983 6363
Stila • 0870 034 2566
StriVectin • 0870 837 7377/Selfridges
Superdrug • 0208 684 7000 • www.superdrug.com
Terax Crema • www.hqhair.com
Tesco • 0800 505 555
Tisserand • 01273 325 666
Tresemme • available nationwide
Tweezerman • 01730 811 811 • www.tweezerman.com
Twisted Sista Curl Activator • www.radicaldesignltd.co.uk
Universal Contour wrap • 01784 259 988 • www.universalcontourwrap.com

Urban Decay • 08450 70 80 90/Boots • www.urbandecay.com
Vincent Longo • www.vincentlongo.com
Virulite • www.vcs.eu.com
Weight Watchers • www.weightwatchers.co.uk
Weleda • 0115 944 8222
Yves Saint Laurent • 01444 255 700 www.ysl.com

For cosmetic acupuncture by Stephen Langley, visit **The Hale Clinic** in London (0845 0094 171) or the **Anne McDevitt Clinic** in Dublin (01 6777 962).

For more information on treatments and reputable practitioners, contact the **British Association of Aesthetic Plastic Surgeons** (020 7405 2234) www. baaps.org.uk

For general advice call **The Healthcare Commission** helpline 0845 601 3012. www.healthcarecommission.org.uk

Ceril's website
www.cerilcampbell.com

Ceril's underwear website
www.redcarpetundies.com

The Compact Book of Being

Beautiful

Jane Cunningham

THE COMPACT BOOK OF BEING BEAUTIFUL

Jane Cunningham

£4.99

ISBN: 1 84024 430 5

ISBN 13: 978 1 84024 430 4

Think sitting pretty is the reserve of the premiere-going princesses? Think again! This book provides straightforward advice on using everyday essentials to buff up your beauty spots to celebrity standard. With everything from basic beauty do's and don'ts to step-by-step tips and make-up artists' secrets, this gorgeous guide will leave you looking and feeling fresh-faced and fabulous!

Jane Cunningham is a journalist and writes for several national newspapers on the subject of beauty.

'a so superbly woven tale that putting it down would cause heartache'

malachy mccourt

The Local

A PUB, A TOWN AND THE SEARCH FOR WHAT MATTERS MOST

Gwendolyn Bounds

THE LOCAL
A PUB, A TOWN AND THE SEARCH
FOR WHAT MATTERS MOST

Gwendolyn Bounds

£7.99

ISBN: 1 84024 520 4
ISBN13: 978 1 84024 520 2

While searching for a temporary haven following the September 11th attacks, Manhattan journalist Wendy Bounds was delivered by a friend to Guinan's – a tiny Irish pub and general store on the banks of the Hudson River.

Captivated by the charismatic owner of this pub that was the living heart of the village, Bounds became one of the regulars and was quickly swept up by its charms and motley characters, including the garrulous Jim Guinan himself, with ailing health but rich tales of the pub's past, and Lou-Lou, the faithful four-legged regular.

A stunning slice of life told with sensitivity and humour, The Local is a love story about a place – and the people who bring it to life. Filled with stories of joy and sorrow, of universal family struggles with loyalty and love, it is a riveting tale of the pub's fight to endure and Bounds's search for a simpler way of life. This beautifully written and brilliantly insightful book is as much about remembering to value the past as it is about learning to seize the present.

Gwendolyn Bounds is an award-winning columnist for the Wall Street Journal.

REAL-LIFE
DIET TIPS

SLIMMING SECRETS THAT REALLY WORK